THE STRENGTHENING OF AMERICAN POLITICAL INSTITUTIONS

The Strengthening of American Political Institutions

✸

A. S. MIKE MONRONEY

THOMAS J. HARGRAVE

THURMAN ARNOLD

ARTHUR E. SUTHERLAND, Jr.

DON K. PRICE

EDGAR ANSEL MOWRER

✸

Cornell University Press

ITHACA, NEW YORK, 1949

23656

tions" was suggested as a subject by the work of Mr. Herbert Hoover's Commission on the Organization of the Executive Branch and by the many other programs and projects of governmental and administrative reform which have recently been presented to the American public. The selection of specific topics—the reorganization of Congress, plans for the mobilization of industry, the federal loyalty program, the reduction of the presidential burden, and the rationalization of foreign policy—was conditioned both by the nature of the audience to which the Symposium was directed and the interest of the faculty and students most concerned. Each speaker was asked to discuss his special topic critically and freely and to give, at least in general terms, an answer to the question of whether or not the proposed reform would lead to the strengthening of our political institutions. The answers of these distinguished public servants record here a critical summary of the state of governmental reform in the year 1949.

On behalf of the University, the Committee wishes to thank the Carnegie Corporation for the generous grant that made the Symposium possible; for itself the Committee wishes to express gratitude to the many members of the University whose advice, encouragement, and assistance made the development of the program practical. It thanks President Day and Provost de Kiewiet for the complete freedom they granted when they delegated this assignment and the generous manner in which they responded to all requests for aid. It also thanks the members of the Department of Government, and particularly Professor Robert Cushman, who assisted the Committee at every step from the formulation of the plans through the actual presentation of the lectures. Finally, the Committee wishes to express its gratitude to the contributors to this volume for far exceeding any formal obligations in their efforts to make the Symposium a success.

Earl Brooks
Clinton L. Rossiter
Edward W. Fox, *Chairman*

Ithaca, New York
June, 1949

❦ Contents

[ix]

1

The Legislative

Reorganization Act of 1946:

A First Appraisal

❦

❧ By A. S. Mike Monroney[*]

FOR one hundred and sixty years Congress has been the butt of more jokes than has any other branch of our government. Certainly we have furnished more cartoon material and have been viewed with alarm in more editorials than has any other organ of local, state, or national government. Not only the public but members of Congress themselves like to jest about our organization. The standard way for a Congressman to begin a speech is to recount how the chaplain of the House invariably opens the session by looking out at the members and then praying for the safety of the country.

As a member of Congress I rather like the humor, most of it good-natured, with which we are treated. I think it tends to prove that we are in reality the peoples' branch of government. If the people stop worrying about us, stop deriding us about our foibles, then I will be greatly concerned. That would mean that the people had come to the conclusion that our importance to democracy had ended.

The records of all our eighty Congresses reveal that the members of Congress themselves have always been

* Representative A. S. Mike Monroney of Oklahoma was Vice-Chairman of the Joint Committee on the Organization of Congress that drafted the Legislative Reorganization Act of 1946, popularly known as the La Follette-Monroney Act.

as much concerned with the institution as have the people. Some of these old speeches make good reading for the present time, for they tell those members who despair over the ability of the Congress to do its job that others have despaired before them! There is always a tendency to bemoan the fact that the giants of former days who walked the halls of the Capitol are found no longer in our membership. I wonder. My own feeling is that the general level of membership in Congress has been improving all through our one hundred and sixty years, and that perhaps those great men of history we read about were prominent partly by comparison with colleagues of lesser ability. And surely the problems that most of the Congresses then confronted were hardly comparable to the tasks that face us today.

If, as I believe, we have demonstrated in this country through all these years that democracy can work, then I think that a good part of the credit must go to Congress. If you read over the Constitution, you will find that the framers of that document vested most of their hopes in the representative system. Congress is mentioned more often and is given more importance than either of the other two divisions of our government. And even today you will find Congress mentioned more often in the daily and Sunday newspapers and on the radio than are the other two branches of government.

Of course, Congress does not run smoothly—or even efficiently. The business of the Congress is to try to resolve the vast disagreements of our people over government policies and programs. We must make up our collective minds in a goldfish bowl, under the most pitiless glare of publicity that the world has ever seen. Every fault, every error, and every disagreement are big news. A totalitarian state with a supine puppet legislature would surely look better and would certainly do its business with more dispatch, but it would be according to the rule of the dictator. Therefore, though we sometimes lose patience with our Congress, with its delays and debates, I think we should realize that the process of democracy requires time and care, give and take, if we are to avoid the loss of our freedom.

The Constitution intended that the Congress should be the branch closest to the people. That is why the House comes up for election every two years. That is why it can be completely changed by the people if they do not like what we have done. It is in fact a part of "neighborhood government." In most congressional districts the change of a mere few thousand votes can change the membership of the House for any good reason, for any bad reason, or for no reason at all. Here the individual's vote becomes most effective. It is many times more important in a congressional election than when submerged as an infinitesimal part of some forty-eight million votes cast in a presidential election.

I think that, on the record, ninety-nine out of a hundred citizens of the United States want to keep a strong Congress in the picture in this democracy of ours. I think that about that many want the best possible Congress they can obtain, that they want us to do our work well, to perform our tasks as effectively as possible. Yet our problems today, instead of being those of thirteen small and rural states, are the problems of furnishing leadership for the democratic world. Not only do the hopes of all free peoples rest on us, but their security, their freedoms, and their economies are definitely linked to the kind of task that we perform.

Because of the tremendous job before us, involving the future of the world, I do not think either Congress or the public can or should be satisfied with ineffectiveness and irresponsibility in the legislative branch. We must keep the true values that flow from a representative system, but we must insist that Congress equip and organize itself to do, in this complex day and age, the job the Constitution demanded that it do. It used to be easy for Congress to meet three or four months a year, pass a few appropriation bills totaling under a billion dollars, decide such momentous questions as which cities and towns would get new post office buildings or which rivers and harbors would be deepened, perhaps tinker with the tariff a bit, and then go home for eight or nine months.

Contrast the difference in the work load today. We must handle the problems of the world's largest and most complex organization, one hundred times bigger than General Motors, United States Steel, and the Pennsylvania Railroad rolled together. Not only must we finance a record-breaking budget of nearly forty-two billion dollars, but we must handle the greatest debt structure ever carried by any government in the world's history. We must implement and assist in carrying out one of the greatest struggles in history between free men and those who would reduce the world to the tyranny of the dark ages. We must provide security, not only for ourselves, but for free people elsewhere in the world who wish to remain free. We must help to plan and approve such military preparation as is needed for that job. We must help in the rebuilding needed because of the devastation of World War II and furnish materials and tools for the strengthening of other nations and for the reconstruction of their shattered economies. We must keep America economically strong, for the task of world leadership cannot be performed if business collapses here. Complex problems of prices, supplies, employment, gross national production, and development of natural resources all have to be studied and resolved in Congress. Is it any wonder that everyone who wants the representative system to survive is greatly concerned with the ability of our system to carry this tremendous work load?

Methods that were satisfactory in the gay nineties are no longer sufficient to today's tasks. Organization and practices and procedures that in those days would carry the insignificant work load of Congress are now as obsolete as a quill pen and old-fashioned cash ledger would be for a great chain-store organization. More important still, the lessons of the past point out clearly that, lacking adequate organization and staff, Congress cannot carry out its tasks under the Constitution. Without the right sort of equipment and procedures it must abdicate its job to the executive department without carefully considering or understanding what this surrender involves. But abdication is not the only danger. Blind, unreasoning, and uninformed obstruction can be just as dangerous. With proper staffing and organization Congress can be effective and can avoid both these dangers—that of being just a rubber stamp and that of being a collection of blind obstructionists.

It was on this basis that the Committee on the Organization of Congress was set up in 1945 and made its report a year later. The original draft of the reorganization bill sought to make it possible for the Congress to handle the problems of 1946–1948. There was no plan for any revolutionary change or departure from the ideas of representative government. It was only to strengthen the hand of the representative system through better organization and equipment that the Legislative Reorganization Act of 1946 was drafted. Generally speaking, our purposes were three in number:

1. To modernize and streamline Congress through the reorganization of its committee structure. This overlapping, duplicating, crazy-quilt system had, like Topsy, just "growed." Committees were added to committees, and the structure grew without plan or program. Under the reorganization bill, the sprawling structure of the House committees was reduced from forty-eight to nineteen, of the Senate from thirty-three to fifteen.

2. To give Congress the staff it needed to handle present-day problems. We sought to give each of the reorganized committees four experts, at salaries large enough to attract qualified and experienced research and professional aides. We also provided for greatly enlarged research staffs in the Legislative Reference Service of the Library of Congress, and we authorized a greatly expanded bill-drafting service.

3. To assist Congress in handling the nation's fiscal affairs, to give better and more effective control of the nation's purse strings, and to provide for over-all consideration of the nation's income and expenditures through the legislative budget. Standardized accounting

procedures, sounder staff work, and many other fiscal reforms were provided for in the act. The failure of the Congress to use many of the fiscal reforms to an effective degree has been the biggest disappointment of reorganization.

I should like now to outline and discuss in more detail the most important of the reforms undertaken by the act, with special reference to the manner in which they are working after two years' experience.

The keystone of the reorganization of Congress was the reorganization of the committees. The committees are the workshops of Congress. At least 80 per cent of the work of Congress is done in them, and the degree of their success in working out all bills determines the quality of our legislative product. In spite of all predictions that a streamlining of the committee structure on a functional rather than historical basis would fail, the new committee organization has stood up well under the test of two years. Reduction of the forty-nine committees of the House to nineteen has failed to overload any of the reorganized committees, with perhaps the single exception of the Judiciary Committee. The Senate, likewise, has not found its committees so overloaded as predicted, despite the reduction from thirty-three to fifteen. Instead of serving on from five to nine separate and divergent committees, each Senator now serves on only two standing committees. Generally, each House member serves on only one, instead of from three to five as many members did in the past. Even though many Senators and House members now hold membership on several subcommittees, their work is largely specialized along one general line, not along five to nine unrelated lines.

The principal complaint against the reorganized committee structure has been that too many subcommittees have grown up. This is partly true. Undoubtedly, without the benefit of experience under the new committee structure, too many such subcommittees were set up in the Eightieth Congress. Experience, however, is tending to reduce this number in the Eighty-first Congress. A partial check of House committees reveals that a substantial reduction is being made in the number of subcommittees. For example, the Armed Services Committee, which reported eleven during the Eightieth Congress, will now use only three. The appropriations subcommittees, which numbered twelve, are now nine; the Judiciary Committee has cut subcommittees down from eight to four. Other committees are using subcommittees only for temporary tasks or assignments. It is thus apparent that the committee structure, which formerly was so overlapping and cumbersome as to destroy the efficiency of congressional action at the committee level, is conforming closely to the reorganization plans.

One of the major gains in relation to the committee structure has been the reduction in the number of special committees. Before reorganization these special committees were established without regard to the duplication of the work of the regular standing committees. In the Seventy-ninth Congress, before reorganization, we had twelve. In the Eightieth the number was reduced to seven. So far this year the Senate has refused to set up any special committees, and the House has passed a resolution to establish only one—a special committee on small business. Under the Reorganization Act, special committees were not prohibited, but their establishment was discouraged on the grounds that regular standing committees had adequate jurisdiction and staff to handle any specialized investigation required. The standing committees also have the power to bring in corrective legislation if any is required, while the special committees can only report and recommend, leaving the actual work still up to the regular legislative committee having jurisdiction.

One important recommendation made in the reorganization plans was that the standing committees be required to carry on "legislative surveillance" of the departments and agencies over which they had jurisdiction. This was to keep the representatives better informed as to the day-to-day work of the departments and agencies and to provide a formal relationship between the executive agencies and Congress. Through better understanding, on the part of the agencies, of the intent of Congress, and with members of Congress in their turn understanding better the work of the agencies, this plan was expected to improve sharply the quality of congressional-executive relationships.

Because of the heavy work load shouldered by the Eightieth Congress, and thus far by the Eighty-first as well, only a few of the standing committees have held these regular report sessions. Those that have used this technique report excellent results, but unfortunately not all committees have reserved a portion of their time for this very important function. Therefore, true legislative surveillance is given only to those agencies that come

[11]

before the Congress during the working out of legislation.

Improvements have been attained along other lines. For example, the number of jurisdictional disputes, which used to require the time of Congress to settle, has been greatly reduced, and only in rare instances has the issue been taken to the floor of either house. This may be attributed to the reduction in the number of committees and to a clearer set of rules of committee jurisdiction. Committee procedures have also been improved. Now, since each committee must have regular meeting days, the meetings are not held merely at the whim of the committee chairman. Moreover, once the committee is in regular session, the majority determines action, thus limiting to some extent the power formerly exercised by a few chairmen. Records of all committee meetings must be kept, together with votes of members. Another improvement in committee rules provides that the chairman must report any measure passed by his committee promptly to the House. An actual quorum must be present at any committee session when legislation is to be reported to the House. Witnesses are required to file written statements in advance of their appearance so that committee members can question them more fully in the hearings. This has tended to eliminate long-winded rambling and time-consuming testimony before committees.

All committees were required by the act to conduct open, public hearings when taking evidence on legislation and appropriations. This has worked well except in one instance. The Appropriations Committee of the House has been stubborn about complying with this provision of the act and has refused to abide by its clear directive. Surely the interest of the public in the cost of government should require this committee to hold open hearings, as departments and others make their case for the next year's appropriations.

Offices of the committees, which formerly were operated as combination congressional offices and committee headquarters, were ordered separated. Now all committee records and business are handled in entirely separate offices. Committee staffs, which formerly divided their time between committee work and work of the members' home districts, now work exclusively on committee business.

The reorganization act has been largely successful in preventing completely new bills from being written by House and Senate conferees and then pushed through both houses under the special privilege procedure granted conference reports. Now only matters in actual disagreement are subject to compromise. Formerly, by a parliamentary maneuver, the entire subject matter could be considered to be in disagreement between the two houses.

Measured on the whole, the reforms contained in the committee reorganization have worked well. I believe any informed critic would appraise the working of this keystone of reorganization as at least a 90 per cent success. The reorganization of the committees was thought to be the most difficult part of the plan, and the fact that it has stood up under two sessions of Congress—and under both Republican and Democratic leaderships— marks its success. Much more improvement needs to be achieved at the committee level as to efficiency, better use of committee time, and more careful consideration of bills after hearings are completed, but these gains can be secured only through harder work by committee chairmen and members and by more experienced staff work.

The second main goal in the reorganization of Congress was to give the houses, and particularly their committees, a skilled professional staff. Before reorganization most committees limped along with completely inadequate staffs. For example, my Banking and Currency Committee, which in the Seventy-ninth Congress handled lending authority for RFC, the Export-Import Bank, the Bretton Woods proposals, and the British loan, totaling some ten billion dollars, did its work with one staff member and two stenographers. The former was paid at the rate of $2,400 a year. This lack of trained assistants to help the committee in the handling of vast and difficult economic problems was certainly penny-wise and pound-foolish.

Because of extreme demands on the member's time made by problems affecting his home district, professional and expert help is of vital importance. Under reorganization we authorized the employment of four professional experts for each of the reorganized committees and provided for pay scales reaching $10,000 per year. In addition, we authorized the doubling of appropriations for the Legislative Reference Service in the Library of Congress. Further increases of $150,000 a year for the following two years were also authorized. Thus we sought to improve the staffing of the Congress, both at the committee level and in terms of an over-all research staff of ample size and experience within the Library of Congress. The committee staffs confine themselves to helping the committee members to specialize on the problems before them. They can and do call on the Legislative Reference Service, however, and an interchange of information and research is maintained between them. Individual members, seeking specialized information and research on difficult subjects, can now avail themselves of this service. The improvement of the Legislative Reference Service in the Library of Congress has been excellent, except that funds for its expansion have not been granted as generously as authorized in the act. The quality of the work done by this service and its complete divorce from political patronage in the recruitment of specialists in many governmental fields has been outstanding.

Less successful has been our experience with the expert staffing of the standing committees of Congress. For the most part, however, the authority to employ high-level, skilled personnel has not been abused by the committees, and there are a great many fine examples of the proper execution of the intent of the act. In some few instances, appointments have been made of unqualified personnel, but criticism both in the Congress and in the press has tended to police this provision. Originally the act contained provision for a congressional personnel director, who was to pass upon the qualifications of all such experts, but this was stricken out of the bill in the Senate. Despite that loss, I believe the general level of qualification of the staff aides is approaching the goal of the bill. The relatively few personnel changes made when control of the House shifted with the Eighty-first

Congress indicated that only in a few isolated instances were political considerations involved in these staff jobs.

I believe that the greatest failure so far in utilizing staff work of both committee employees and Legislative Reference Service employees may be ascribed to the failure of members to rely on staff work. Members have had to operate for so many years without any such help that they are reluctant to assign jobs to their experts. Undoubtedly, as the staffs become more experienced in their work, and the members become more experienced in relying on them, this process of utilizing staff work will prove a great aid to improving our capacity to do our job. No one can doubt or question the need that we have for our own fact-finders. Congress is bombarded by a multiplicity of statistical material, and by alleged research data and so-called facts offered it by pressure groups from outside government and from various departments within. We need, and must have, reliable statistical data on which we can depend when making important decisions. Only an independent staff of our own, such as was provided for in the act, can make this possible.

Another innovation was the enlargement of the Office of the Legislative Counsel. Surely one of the principal jobs of Congress is to write its own legislation. Yet experience has shown that an extremely high percentage of the legislation considered is drafted elsewhere than on Capitol Hill. The need for independent drafting of legislation is obvious. Many obscure passages may be placed in long and complex bills, which despite a careful combing out by the congressional committees, might still permit misinterpretation or authorize something that Congress did not intend. The best way to prevent any jokers from getting into legislation is to provide for all bills to be drafted by our own Legislative Counsel. This improvement, because of the fine career service that has always obtained in that office, has made it possible for committees and individual members to obtain much better service in the drafting of legislation. Still, much is to be desired, for altogether too often Congress has for consideration measures drafted outside of Congress by departments or agencies, whereas it should require that every sentence and every phrase be drafted or checked on Capitol Hill.

The provision for executive assistants for members of the Senate was incorporated in a separate bill, although such assistants had originally been provided for both House and Senate members. Unquestionably, the Senate had greater need for these experts than the House, by reason of the heavier work load that it carries. This provision, which relieves the Senator of many of the smaller details of his office by providing for a skilled assistant, is proving of great value.

Taking the entire results into consideration, my estimate of the success of this effort to improve our staffing would be to rate it at about 75 per cent of our goal. I believe, however, that the trend is in the direction of better and more efficient staffing and that experience will tend to increase, rather than decrease, this percentage of success.

The most complete and dismal failure of reorganization is in the field of more effective fiscal control. This was one of our principal goals and surely one of the most needed. Control of the financial affairs of an enterprise of the size of this government, with about forty-two billion dollars of expenditures each year, is the biggest undertaking of Congress. It was our hope that through reorganization and improvement of the mechanics of budgetary control, improved accounting methods, better staffing, and complete modernization, some of the management efficiency of large commercial organizations could be utilized in Congress and in our appropriation techniques. Instead, we are operating in virtually the same way as we did when the federal budget was less than one-tenth of what it is today. I have often heard the reorganization bill accused of failure because these fiscal provisions have not worked out. Most of them have never yet been actually tried.

The most conspicuous failure under the fiscal control provisions of the act has been the legislative budget. This provision required Congress to prepare its own budget in the early part of each session, estimating both income and expenditures through the joint action of the revenue-raising and revenue-spending committees of both houses. Previously appropriations had been made without reference to any over-all total and with the revenue-raising committees completely ignored as to how much money was required to be raised. It was to avoid this hermetically sealed vacuum of the two fiscal committees of each house that the legislative budget was authorized.

The Eightieth Congress made a stab at the legislative budget, but at best it was a hasty guess. The House resolved to reduce the President's budget by $6,000,000,-000, and the Senate resolved to reduce it by $4,500,-

000,000. They never got the bill out of conference. The following year, both houses agreed on a reduction of $2,500,000,000, which failed completely to approximate the total spent. This year the Congress first agreed to postpone the date of the legislative budget until May 1 in an effort to put enough work on this provision to establish a reliable budget in line with income and expected expenditures, and then it abandoned this part of the Legislative Reorganization Act completely. This, I believe, was a most unfortunate decision as well as a keen disappointment for all those members interested in adequate, responsible fiscal control by Congress.

The hostility of the leaders of the appropriations committees to the idea of binding themselves by the adoption of a legislative budget has been so intense that it is difficult to achieve any sort of enthusiastic cooperation on this important provision. Even a poor performance in the handling of the budget, however, is better than no effort at all. The attendant public discussion of income and outgo that takes place marks the only time during the session of Congress that the two important ends of the purse strings, income and expenditures, are effectively tied together. The budget provisions could work if these leaders wished to make them work. It would require an excellent staff of skilled accountants, working during the fall and winter on a study of all departmental budgets as they were made up. The staff would have to follow these budgets through the Bureau of the Budget and know all of the expenditures in detail. By giving the committee the advantage of their continuing study, the staff would assume the presentation of a budget that would then be something more than a mere guess.

Originally the act provided for the assignment of four experts to each of the appropriations subcommittees. At present there are nine subcommittees in the House, with opposite numbers in the Senate. The appropriations committees fought against this improved staffing, and at their request were given blanket authorization to employ such experts as they needed. Despite the growing size of the federal budget and the complexity of national and international expenditures, these committees have maintained extremely small staffs. In the House only ten genuine experts are employed, along with two men on the investigatory staff. Additional part-time investigators and auditors are sometimes employed, but on a per-diem basis. Based on a forty-two-billion-dollar budget, this signifies a work load for the staff of more than three billion dollars per staff member. No one can question the ability of those employed, but I feel that a greatly enlarged staff would enable the committee to ferret out of the money bills much more information and facts regarding the agencies than is now done with the small staffs used. Only by more and better information on every appropriation item in the budget can the ever-increasing expenditures of government be reduced. A larger staff would at least permit on-the-ground investigations and studies of operations of many of the more expensive departments and would result in much economy.

Another provision of the act provided for expenditure analyses of government departments by the comptroller general. This was "to enable Congress to determine whether public funds have been economically and efficiently administered and expended." While the comptroller general makes informal reports to this end, the money that has been asked to expand this study has so far been denied by the Appropriations Committee.

Another section of the act was completed in January of 1949 when the comptroller general reported on useless restrictions which have in the past been incorporated into appropriations bills. Many are so obsolete that the cost of the paper work far exceeds any possible savings. This report will probably result in the dropping of many of the obsolete restrictions which have been carried over from year to year in the appropriation bills.

Some progress has been made in preventing legislation on appropriation bills. The rule is observed rather strictly in the House, but despite this care statutory changes framed in the guise of restricting appropriations often creep in. These violations of the spirit of the House rules, however, have lessened to a considerable degree.

Another improvement which has been generally successful is the requirement that appropriation bills be reported to the House at least three days before they are considered. This gives the members and the press a better chance to study and analyze the bills before they are called up. In the past most bills were reported to the House and taken up immediately.

Some progress is being made by the comptroller general in the establishment of an "integrated accounting system" for all federal agencies. At present it is most difficult to harmonize accounts and totals between Congress, the Budget Bureau, the Treasury, and the General

Accounting Office. The adoption of such a standardized or integrated system, which will reveal in "showcase" fashion the principal items of expenditures for all government departments and agencies, will do much to promote efficiency and economy. Officials of the Treasury and other agencies have been working for more than a year in an effort to simplify and standardize these accounting procedures, as provided for in the act.

Despite the clear mandate of the act, the House Appropriations Committee hearings remain closed to the public, and it is doubtful if they will be opened as long as the committee is controlled by the present leaders. Little has been done also on the requirement for a study of the permanent appropriations authorized by previous Congresses in order to determine whether any of those recurring items could be eliminated or should be subjected to annual review.

While I would not list it as one of the three leading objectives of reorganization, surely the effort to persuade Congress to rid itself of time-consuming and inconsequential details was of great importance. We recommended the delegation of power to settle private claim bills to the courts, and the power to alter Army and Navy records to civilian review boards, and in other ways we sought to pass on these minor duties to duly constituted agencies, in order to reserve as much time as possible for matters properly demanding the attention of the national legislature. So far this reform has worked only partially, with too many private bills still before Congress and with a multitude of private immigration matters still clogging up the Judiciary Committee. A general bill is needed to remove both of these duties to courts and administrative agencies, where they could be handled better. The refusal of Congress to hand over to the City of Washington the job of running District of Columbia affairs also has continued this extraneous work load. If Congress is to be more efficient, it must realize that it cannot pay attention to all kinds of insignificant detail. It must reserve its attention to matters genuinely affecting national affairs and national policies.

Other features of the act are working reasonably well, although several need still more improvement. The Lobby Registration Act, which has resulted in 1,561 registrations by lobbyists and organizations, has served to indicate the amount of lobbying activity that goes on. It is an incomplete and inaccurate record, however, and the act badly needs tightening up to furnish more accurate information on these activities.

Included in the reorganization bill were provisions for an increase in congressional salaries from $10,000 per year to $12,500, plus a $2,500 tax-free expense allowance. Members also were granted the privilege of joining the federal retirement system if they chose, by paying into the retirement fund at the rate of 6 per cent of their salaries. Retirement is provided at sixty-two, based on the length of congressional service. A member, to be eligible, must have served for at least five years. Since no complaint about the effectiveness of these provisions of reorganization has been voiced from the membership, it can be assumed that they are working as planned. It was thought that many of the more elderly members would take advantage of the retirement features and thus open the way to service by younger men. This has not occurred yet to any marked degree, however, and dozens of members, long past the permitted retirement age, continue to serve.

The *Congressional Record* has been greatly improved by the addition of daily indexes, summaries of the day's activities in both houses and their committees, and other useful data. Minor improvements in the physical plant at the Capitol and other incidental improvements have also taken place.

My evaluation of the over-all success of reorganization, based on a contrast of what we hoped to do and what has actually been done, would be to score the entire program at a bare 51 per cent. Time may improve this score, as more of the provisions of the act are put into actual force and more pains are taken to make them work.

It was a great disappointment, both to me and to many political scientists, that the Committee on the Organization of Congress could not do something about the three principal difficulties that handicapped congressional improvement—seniority, the veto power of the House Rules Committee, and the filibuster in the Senate. Although we were denied the right to deal with these traditional obstructions, I have always felt that the improvement of Congress along other lines would help to spotlight and eventually to help correct them.

The action of the House at the start of this session in removing the absolute veto power of the Rules Committee over legislation reported by the standing committees marks a great deal of progress. I believe that the change in the rules to permit the House itself to override a Rules Committee veto of a bill will enable most committees to get their legislation to the floor. In the past the power of the Rules Committee was so great that it was able not only to deny a rule for consideration of the bill, but, as in the Eightieth Congress, to insist that a standing coequal committee of the House change a bill to conform to the Rules Committee's desires. The removal of this power surely will help to eliminate one of the three principal road blocks obstructing Congress.

The second obstruction, the Senate filibuster, seems now to be more firmly entrenched than ever before. I would scarcely care to hazard a guess as to when an effective cloture rule can finally be established.

The last and hardest remaining obstruction is the seniority rule. It is difficult to repeal an unwritten rule that is deeply cemented into the processes of both houses. Not only does this seniority rule protect the chairmen of the committees, but, after a few short years of service, every member of both bodies becomes aware that the system gives him certain standing privileges and a position on committees that he might not otherwise have.

One hope that something might be done in the future lies in the fact that the last election proved that an aggressive campaign could dramatize party responsibility and accountability for the actions of the party controlling Congress. If it worked on the Eightieth Congress, it can work on the Eighty-first or the Eighty-second. One of the chief difficulties in the path of any correction of this obsolete system of choosing congressional executives, however, is the lack of a ready and foolproof system to take its place. The alternative of election of chairmen by the committees themselves is filled with dangers of creating long-lasting schisms among the majority-party committee members. The alternative of choosing the chairmen by a genuine vote of the House— instead of a *pro forma* vote as is now done—offers a chance for a good back-slapper to take over the chairmanship or to throw the House into a logrolling system of state alignments. Appointment by the Speaker, as was done many years ago, goes back to creating czaristic powers in the Speaker. One of the best suggestions, but still far from perfect, is the suggestion for rotating the chairmanship every four years among the members having the greatest seniority. If Congress would adopt the proposal made in the original reorganization bill for majority and minority policy committees, and make these policy committees truly representative of the finest talent available in the Congress, this job could best be left to this group.

One of the great needs of the Congress is the formation of real majority and minority policy committees in both houses. Under the proposal, the policy committees of each house would have been elected by the parties at the beginning of each session, and membership on them would have automatically terminated at the end of the session. It was our idea that in this type of executive committee, reflecting the will of the recently elected members, each Congress would not be bound by the seniority of the past, at least on these policy committees. Each session the committee would vest in the elected members considerable responsibility for the leadership of the parties for that session of Congress. Particularly would this be true in relationship to the majority policy committees. They would have had the right to advise and guide the entire majority policy, scheduling legislation, publicly expressing the official party position on measures, and bringing party accountability and responsibility to bear upon the program in Congress.

It was further planned that the majority policy committees of the House and Senate, acting jointly, would serve as a formal council to meet regularly with the President to facilitate the formation of national policy and to improve the relationship between the executive and legislative branches of government. This provision was stricken out of the bill when it came to the House, and only the Senate policy committees were established under later legislation. This half-a-loaf treatment of the policy committee proposal has not worked out as well as intended. The authority and the leadership of the Senate policy committees have been weakened because there is no counterpart for them in the House machinery. Sooner or later Congress, if it is to fulfill its obligations, must improve its organization, particularly at the policy level, in order to give direction to a well-rounded and complete program.

In summary, I believe the remainder of our task in strengthening Congress requires: (1) change of the seniority system for committee chairmanships; (2) improvement of methods and techniques in the handling of fiscal affairs; (3) elimination of the filibuster in the Senate; (4) strengthening party responsibility and accountability through real and effective majority and minority policy committees in both houses; (5) removing from Congress as much of the nonlegislative and extraneous work load as possible.

[27]

Since the effectiveness of committee work is the most important function in improving congressional action, a limited term as chairman of a committee would spur the incumbent to faster action and a desire for achievement of legislative goals before his term expires. Old age, which so often is synonymous with length of service in Congress, would no longer be a handicap if some other method of selection were employed, such as election by the majority policy committee of either House. And yet I am frank to admit that this change away from seniority is the most difficult, if not impossible, task that the Congress has to face. No one can deny the advantage of experience and training on these committees, but to permit any chairman to hold office for a span of twenty years, denying this opportunity to others who have served for ten to twelve years, seems to me to be defeating our democratic processes.

I would place the greatly needed improvement in the handling of our fiscal affairs as second on the list in building a more effective Congress. Half the job of the Congress is in wielding the powers of the purse. The inspecting and checking that should go on in the granting of appropriations is one of the greatest forces in congressional control, if properly used. Improved staffing to make Congress the master of the purse strings in reality as well as in name would do much to improve our democratic processes. The more vigilant the care that is used in on-the-scene studies of governmental operations, the more exacting the screening of requests for funds; and the more effective the requirements for the stewardship of these funds, the more efficient and responsible will be the fiscal management of our government. Better problems, complaints, letters from constituents, visits, and conferences with groups from the home state or groups interested in legislation—all cut down on the time that members ought to devote to the study and understanding of legislation. While delegation of unimportant or administrative functions to other agencies has helped some, the demands upon the time of the average Senator and member of Congress still leaves far too little time for his real legislative job. It probably will require additional staff help to remove a part of this work load from the member, but even the best assistant cannot free him completely for his legislative duties. Here is one of the ways in which Congress could be greatly improved if the means were found for solving this riddle. Former Representative Ramspeck suggested that the Congress be divided into halves, with one half of each state delegation serving as errand boys and Washington contactmen, and the other half serving as real legislators and devoting their time exclusively to this end. This proposal met with no favor from members, however, for all realized that the service-giving branch would find reelection easy, while the voting member, without the contacts, would find election almost impossible!

I have spoken at length about our weaknesses and only briefly about our strength. I do feel that the Congress does a much better job of resolving our differences and maintaining its proper position in our democracy than is generally conceded. Granted that we do not always complete action on every piece of legislation desired, or that our legislation, when completed, is not always perfect. Surely it is never unanimously approved by all the people. Progress in a democracy is never complete, and people never unanimously agree on any issue. But in the long run I feel that Congress represents the will of the majority and that it reflects endless hours of work and consideration with a keen understanding of most of the problems involved, no matter how complex the legislation. I feel also that the average Congressman wants to do a good job in serving his country, and that he is jealous of maintaining the rightful place and power of the legislative branch.

Elsewhere, in almost every country of the world, the parliamentary system has failed. In countries where dictators have taken over, it has always been because the parliamentary systems have proved their inability to cope with the complex and difficult problems that face modern society. That is the real significance of congressional reorganization. An effective and efficient Congress is our first bulwark against dictatorship and the leading institution we have today to protect our liberties and our democracy.

2

America Must Be Ready:
The Problem of Industrial
Mobilization

❧ By Thomas J. Hargrave *

AMERICA is preparing her house for peace—or war. That sounds paradoxical; but is it? Peace will be the invited guest, but war may crash the party. That has occurred before, most unexpectedly, when we Americans were not prepared in advance for the crash.

One of our wisest men, Bernard M. Baruch, in an address before the Industrial College of the Armed Services, declared, "My experience in two world wars, their aftermaths, and the endeavors to make a lasting peace makes me marvel at the regularity with which errors are repeated."

Mr. Baruch continued, "One of the errors that most frequently recurs is failure to study and understand the records of past experience. . . . We must not again make the mistake of not being properly organized in case another war is thrust upon us. . . . With the new instrumentalities of mass destruction, we shall not have time to improvise."

Mr. Baruch has been urging for thirty years that we heed the lessons of experience, ever since he served as

---

* Thomas J. Hargrave, President of the Eastman Kodak Company, was captain of a machine gun batallion and winner of the Distinguished Service Cross in the First World War and Chairman of the Munitions Board set up under Title II of the National Security Act of 1947.

chairman of the War Industries Board in the first World War. Yet somehow we could not bring ourselves to believe that the second conflict was coming, or that we would be involved if it did come. Our faith in the oceans was deeper and wider than their waters. But now we see plainly. We see that what happens anywhere is of concern everywhere.

There could be a third World War. That is a dreadful thought. I do not think war is inevitable. It may not even be likely. But in this troubled world of desperately conflicting ideologies, our country—while working and paying and praying for peace—must be ready for any emergency. I cannot assess, because I do not know, the extent of any threat to our liberty and our way of life; but clearly a potential threat exists. By being ready to meet it we may be able to stop it. It was George Washington himself who said to the Congress, on January 8, 1790, "To be prepared for war is one of the most effectual means of preserving peace."

In this age of mechanized war, planning for industrial preparedness is absolutely essential. Modern war is fought by men, but *with* machines. Men alone cannot win. I should like to write about the courage and valor of our men, but this article must necessarily be about industry and machines. The victor in any coming war must have the most and the best machines. Furthermore, "too late" could be more quickly fatal than "too little."

The increased importance of machines in war is shown by the relative cost of munitions. By munitions I mean weapons of all kinds—ships, planes, tanks, guns, ammunition, electronic devices, and almost everything except such items as food, clothing, and housing. In the Franco-Prussian War of 1870, munitions came to about 7 per cent of the total monetary cost. In the first World War that figure moved up to about 35 per cent, and in the second World War it was approximately 75 per cent. Another war would push it higher still.

I should like to discuss the problem of improving our plans for industrial mobilization with special reference to the agency with which I have been most intimately associated, the Munitions Board. The Munitions Board is one of the four agencies created in 1947 by the National Security Act that are responsible to the Secretary of Defense. The other three are the War Council, the Joint Chiefs of Staff, and the Research and Development Board. Two other agencies—the National Security Council and the National Security Resources Board, both of them outside the National Military Establishment and responsible to the President—were created by the same act. The purpose of all these agencies—together, of course, with the Army, Navy, and Air Force—is to protect our country through the creation of a strong military force, aggressive research for and development of new instruments and techniques, erection of a sound intelligence system, imparting of thorough knowledge of all major diplomatic commitments to the military establishment, and a program of industrial preparedness. These are the chief factors that make for national strength. It is of the last of these that I write in this article.

The National Security Resources Board and the Munitions Board are the particular agencies established to apply the lessons of the past to the needs of the future, as they relate to resources and production. Billions of dollars may be saved by planning for industrial preparedness. Vastly more important, tens of thousands of lives may be saved. War itself may be prevented. This entire program indicates that we have learned something from history, that next time—if there has to be a next time—we must get off to a fast start. And it means certain victory if, and only if, we as a nation preserve the moral and spiritual fiber necessary to sustain our faith in our way of life. The main purposes of the Munitions Board in time of peace are the planning of military aspects of industrial mobilization and coordinating the production, procurement, and distribution procedures of the armed forces. Those are the high-sounding words of the statute, but when reduced to action they become fairly simple.

But first, what did we learn from the recent war? In my opinion it is not far short of a miracle that the War Production Board and other agencies of World War II accomplished all that they did. They had no statutory, controlling plan for industrial mobilization such as is being developed now. There had been no systematic contacts with industry, no advance industrial planning on the basis of strategic military plans, no stock-piling worthy of the name. They had to improvise, and in doing so they necessarily stumbled and faltered. Every businessman recalls what happened when the last war broke upon us. There was almost frantic confusion. Everyone wanted to do something, but there was no plan. One production program collided with another. A priority to buy materials soon became little more than

a hunting license. There were *A* priorities, then *A-1* up
to *A-10*, double *A*'s, triple *A*'s, and finally the roof blew
off on all letter and number significance.

Some plants changed from what they had been making to something less essential, but they did not know it.
Locomotive works went to tanks, when locomotives
were more necessary. Truck plants that should have remained just that went in for airplanes. Plant managers,
eager to make good on high-priority contracts, often
ordered—and sometimes got—far more raw materials
than they immediately needed, thus slowing down other
plants with equally high-priority contracts. There simply was not enough to give every manager all he needed,
plus all he wanted for a margin of safety. There was
no adequate plan to apportion critical materials on the
basis of contracts. It was two years before the Controlled
Materials Plan brought order to the allocation of the
most vital raw materials. That plan, proposed by
Ferdinand Eberstadt, was a signal contribution to our
war effort. That plan, or something like it, must be used
again. We must, as Mr. Baruch said, "study and understand the records of past experience."

Among such records, too, was disordered competition
among government buyers for plant capacity. War
orders came to businessmen from many sources, each
one as a rule operating independently of the others and
without knowledge of what the others were doing.
Nearly everyone wanted his order filled by "next Monday." But before next Monday arrived, there would be
other orders equally insistent and perhaps inconsistent
with plant capacity and skills.

The imperative demand for munitions, when war

hits an unprepared nation, makes this sort of confusion and delay inevitable. Last time we did it the hard way, but the all-important fact is that we did it. The driving power of patriotism, the genius of American business, the zeal and ability of wartime officials finally brought us to production peaks that thrilled the Allied world. Our side could not have won without America's industrial achievements.

But it took nearly two years to hit top production. We were lucky, just as in World War I, to have Allies who carried on while we got ready. If the furies of war break loose again, will there be a shield of strong friends between us and the enemy to give us time to do what we should have done earlier? Can we afford or, indeed, survive delay and a disordered start? All of us know what is happening in this uneasy world, and we know the answers to those questions. Two years was a long time in the last war. Two months may be a long time if there is a next. We must make industrial plans now or risk disaster.

These plans, developed by the Munitions Board to be carried forward in co-operation with the entire military establishment and with American business, include the following:

1. A survey of thousands of privately owned plants to learn what they are making and what they might make in an emergency.

2. The preservation in an industrial reserve of more than four hundred specialized munitions plants (built by the government during the last war) ready for quick production.

3. The retention and maintenance of thousands of es-

sential machine tools (used during the last war) in an immediately available reserve.

4. The stock-piling of critical raw materials.

5. The guidance of private companies in making their own internal plans so that plant managers will know the part they are to take in defending this nation and how to do it.

6. The allocation of thousands of industrial plants among the three armed services, so that each service will know where to go first for its munitions needs.

7. A continuing study of military requirements (based on strategic plans of the Joint Chiefs of Staff) in order to determine their production feasibility.

8. The co-ordination of military production, procurement, and distribution.

9. The elimination of duplicate facilities and services by making common use of them by the armed forces.

10. A continuing study of such economic controls, affecting the military establishment, as may become necessary.

These are the most important objectives of the Munitions Board. Here I can give only the "highlights of the highlights" of the tremendous programs involved.

The more than four hundred specialized munitions plants now in our industrial reserve cost the government about six billion dollars to build. They include shipyards, airplane plants, ammunition plants, armament plants, and many others. All were "rescued," with the help of Congress, from the eager postwar rush to demobilize—to liquidate war facilities by scrapping or selling everything in sight. This important program was inaugurated by the former Army and Navy Munitions Board, under the able leadership of Richard R. Deupree, its chairman. At the instance of that board, an excellent survey of such plants was made by Donald M. Nelson, who wrote a strong report to the President recommending that the plants be preserved.

Most of us, you will remember, were then in favor of getting rid of the war and all its works in a hurry. Like boys fresh out of school for the summer, we were ready to throw away our books as if they would never be needed again. A few voices, notably that of Mr. Baruch, were raised in warning, but few listened. We are an optimistic, peace-loving people. Every time we get a war behind us, we hope it will be the final war, and we act as if it would be. Our entire history proves that we have no interest in conquest or empire building and have no desire to indulge in such activities. Some peoples, apparently, do not realize this, but we hope that some day they will. Meanwhile, we should keep on hoping that the last war has been fought. At the same time, we should "keep our atoms dry."

The four hundred reserved industrial plants, mentioned earlier, will be supplemented by a reserve of nearly 200,000 machine tools, originally costing the government about one billion dollars. The machine-tool bottleneck was one of the most serious we confronted in the late war. Such a bottleneck need not and must not happen again.

In addition to preserving specialized munitions plants and machine tools, the Munitions Board has launched a plan for the allocation of privately owned plants among the services. About 80,000 plants, of all kinds and sizes, were engaged in war production during World War II. A survey will cover all of them, but only about 20,000 will be allocated. Up to now, 14,500 plants have been tentatively assigned to one or more of the armed forces. Every plant so allocated will be visited by competent representatives of the Army, Navy, or Air Force. Discussions will be held with plant managers and plans developed so that in case another war comes these plants may move swiftly into production.

It is neither practicable nor necessary to assign all industrial plants in the nation. Many would serve the allocated plants as subcontractors or suppliers, and many would continue to make civilian goods, for civilians must have enough supplies, too. Military forces would distintegrate rapidly if the civilian front collapsed. Plants making what are called "common components"—items necessary for both civilian and military uses, such as bearings, gauges, tires, small electric motors, batteries, compression pumps, generators, internal combustion engines, and numerous other products—would be likely to continue their usual lines. But present thinking is that such plants, as well as those manufacturing machine tools, will, before any national emergency arises, be given large tentative orders— sometimes called "phantom orders"—by some government agency, such as the Reconstruction Finance Corporation, so that they could go into high production as soon as they received the word. A revived War Production Board, or some similar war agency, would thereafter distribute the plant output according to needs.

Co-operation of companies in the plant allocation plan is, of course, voluntary. There is no law, and none is needed, to convince businessmen of the value of this kind of planning. Most of them remember how difficult and costly it was to get into full war production last time. All they wanted last time, all they would want another time, is a clear understanding of what is needed. Given that, they will do the rest. This plant allocation is tentative until the plant manager consents. It does not mean that plants will be "taken over" by the military. It does mean that so much of a plant's capacity as is necessary to turn out a specified schedule of war goods will be assigned for this purpose. Nor is the assignment a "marriage" for the duration of any war. Its principal purpose is to get industry off to a fast, orderly start. The assignment is also bound to stimulate the development of plans by the plants themselves to line up their sources and subcontractors in advance of the day when the first war orders might have to be placed.

I think it should be understood that this comprehensive plan to get set industrially is not the brain child of a few officials. It is not something talked over only in government offices or completed in whispered corridor conferences. It is not something held back for sudden imposition on industry. It is not a bureaucratic strait jacket. It is, instead, the development of co-operative efforts by government and private industry. A total of about 450 businessmen, serving on Munitions Board advisory committees, have helped mightily in putting together a plan that is workable. In addition, the Munitions Board has conferred with numerous other businessmen, including those who held important government positions in the industrial field in the late war. Industrial groups such as in the American Ordnance

Association, the Navy Industrial Association, the Aircraft Industries Association, and several others have been consulted. The Munitions Board is striving for the best business procedures—not by compulsion, but by co-operation. Compulsion is abhorrent to Americans; it is neither necessary nor advisable in a free economy that wants to remain free.

Many businessmen, whose plants have been tentatively allocated to one or more of the armed services, are concerned (and properly so) because they have not yet been approached by them. They are anxious to get their own required advance planning completed as soon as possible. Unfortunately, approaching and conferring with 14,500 plant managers takes time as well as qualified military personnel. My advice to the armed forces is to make such contacts at the earliest possible moment. My advice to the businessmen is to be patient, because the end result—better preparedness for a national emergency—will justify it.

Plants cannot operate without materials, and if we wait until an emergency comes, some essential materials may not be available. That is why the Munitions Board has insisted on adequate stockpiles of sixty-seven critical materials. No war of any considerable duration can be fought without them. The prosperous civilian economy today could be upset by a too swift withdrawal of certain materials from current production. One problem of the Board, therefore, has been to balance current peacetime needs against possible emergency needs in the future. All of the items on the critical list—such as tungsten, manganese, copper, bauxite, tin, zinc, lead,

chromite, coconut oil, pepper, sisal, and industrial diamonds—are used for peaceful purposes, too.

At current prices an adequate stockpile will require
the buying of more than three billion dollars worth of
such critical materials. But whatever the cost now, it
will be far greater if war occurs. Then we would have
to go far for these materials. Most of them are located in
remote parts of the earth such as China, India, Russia,
and Africa. We would have to maintain long sea lanes to
get them here, and we might even have to fight for
them.

My personal conviction is that stock-piling should, in
the case of most items, be limited only by their availabil-
ity. The safest course is to pile up all we can now. This
would not be money spent and gone forever. It would
be money soundly invested. The stockpiles, if not needed
for war, would be useful for future peacetime production. Experience indicates clearly that the value of
critical materials always tends upward. It is not likely
that industrial diamonds, for example, will decrease
much from present value over a long period of time. An
investment in a stockpile now could mean a tremendous
dollar profit, come peace or war, twenty-five years from
now. This is one of the rare chances our government
has to make money.

As an American, stock-piling appeals to me because
it is prudent in the interest of national survival. As a
businessman, it appeals to me as an investment. I hope
others will see it in the same way and not be shocked
if additional large sums of money are appropriated to
buy piles of essential materials. That money will come
back to us in the future. It will never be lost. And while

saving our money, we may at the same time be saving our lives.

How do we know that these materials will be essential in the next war? Is not invention moving along? And are not destructive techniques advancing always and alarmingly? That is true, and the facts are being carefully noted. But there is no probability that the munitions of another war would be wholly different from those formerly used and those of which we have knowledge. Industrial preparedness does not rest complacently on experience of the past. It takes stock of those experiences and goes forward. We are not planning to fight the last war. We are planning for the one we hope never will come, and this very planning may prevent its coming. For all nations know that industrial might is a foundation of victory.

In time of war the United States military establishment becomes the biggest buyer in the world. During three years of World War II our military services bought something more than $147,000,000,000 worth of munitions and supplies. If World War III should occur, the buying would be on an even vaster scale. Can anything be done to make that operation more orderly than heretofore?

The answer is, "Yes." Since the end of the war, and especially since unification of the services, much has been done to put more efficiency in buying. What are called "single service procurement assignments" have been made. This means that one branch of the service—the Army, Navy, or Air Force—is given sole responsibility for buying certain common-use items for all three branches. Already we have legally confirmed or initially placed at least 75 per cent, by dollar volume, of peacetime and wartime buying under single or joint procurement. More such assignments will be made. The joint purchases are petroleum and medical supplies. Instead of competition by one service against another, we shall in most cases have centralized buying. This should be good news not only to taxpayers but to businessmen who may be asked to accept war contracts. For instance, food will be bought by the Army for all services; coal by the Navy; trucks, tanks, and automotive equipment by the Army; combat and landing craft by the Navy; photographic equipment by the Air Force; and so on through the long list.

Obtaining standard specifications for equipment is another big project of the Board. This promises large dividends. The 37,500 electrical and electronic meters —panel instruments—once in use have been reduced to 3,700. Vacuum tube types have been reduced from 3,000 to 195. These and many other similar accomplishments were effected by the able staff of the Army-Navy Electronics and Electrical Standards Agency. That's quite a name—but they lived up to it—in co-operation with the instrument manufacturers and the American Standards Association.

I mention this to indicate what can and will be done. Current projects include plans to standardize engines of all kinds—automotive, internal combustion, industrial, and marine. The Air Force and the air arm of the Navy have already done a magnificent job in standardizing airplane parts and components.

There will also be a common catalogue of items. In

World War II the armed forces handled five million items. Of course, there were not that many different items; but because there were no uniform descriptions, the total number went bewilderingly upward. We should eventually be able to cut that five million figure in half. It is a long program, a three- or four-year one, but well worth the time and cost. Standardization and common catalogues will assure savings in production, transportation, maintenance, storage, and training. This is readily apparent. Not so apparent but just as important is the elimination of duplication of engineering effort and production facilities, both of which are critical in time of war. Another great advantage will be the ready exchangeability of thousands of items between the armed forces.

The armed forces are now publishing uniform procurement regulations, uniform for the first time in history. This means that for all three services there will be uniform contract provisions, uniform inspection procedures, uniform pricing policies, uniform packaging, uniform auditing, and so forth. The advantages of such uniformity, both to the services and to industry, are too obvious to discuss.

There will be common use of many facilities, too. There may now be many separate airfields even when there is no sound reason for them, separate hospitals under circumstances where joint hospitals would serve better, and many other separate facilities, such as offices, cafeterias, laundries, and post exchanges, which can and should be shared by the services if that appears to be the most efficient and economical thing to do. This whole subject is being carefully studied, and considerable progress in the unification of facilities is already being made.

This industrial make-ready program is now being given a practical test. The Joint Chiefs of Staff have developed what is called a strategic plan for defense against an imagined enemy. They have decided where and how to fight a hypothetical war. The role of each branch of the service in such a war has been assigned. In turn, the Army, Navy, and Air Force are breaking down that strategic plan into the munitions and supplies required to carry it out. How many ships, planes, landing craft, tanks, guns, and so on will be needed—and how much steel, copper, and aluminum to make them—is being determined.

The Munitions Board then takes these military requirements and fits them, if they will fit, into the country's industrial potential, both civilian and military. This is done in co-operation with the National Security Resources Board, which has the high responsibility of determining the industrial capacity of the nation for civilian requirements, for other agency requirements such as the Atomic Energy Commission and the Maritime Commission, and for the military requirements, as the latter are computed by the armed services and the Munitions Board. Available raw materials (from stock piles and from domestic sources), available transportation, electric power, fuel, communication facilities, and the like are determined; and if the military requirements for the imagined war do not exceed the possible, the Munitions Board will declare the strategic plan feasible.

If it does, it will then give the green light to the armed services, and their procurement officers in turn can then give to their assigned plant contractors and others a definite answer to their sixty-four-dollar question, namely, the exact kind and amount of any particular munitions needed and the time when needed, the "what, how much, and when" question I have heard so often.

If the capacity of the nation, as determined by the National Security Resources Board, is found to be insufficient to produce the munitions required and also to sustain civilian needs, the strategic plan must be altered or the material requirements of the services modified. This practical workout will be repeated from time to time, and the industrial mobilization plan will be altered as the workouts, new techniques, advancing inventions, or revisions of the strategic plan or concept laid down by the Joint Chiefs of Staff show need for such alteration.

James V. Forrestal, our former Secretary of Defense, deserves the gratitude of all of us for his extraordinary zeal in stimulating action on this practical test of the strategic plan and other industrial planning. Never before in the United States have we done anything like this. Never before have we had industrial preparedness prescribed by law and so carefully planned.

Winston Churchill once described war production in a free economy as resulting first in a trickle, then a stream, and finally a flood. If production for war ever again becomes necessary, we are making ready to begin with a stream and reach flood stage quickly.

Recently, Mr. Churchill said something else. "It is my belief—I say it with deep sorrow—that at the present time the only sure foundation of peace and of the prevention of actual war rests upon strength."

But neither George Washington nor Winston Churchill said that preparedness was the only way to prevent war. Neither accepted the defeatist philosophy that war is inevitable. We must not accept it. We want peace, lasting peace, and we must work for it always. But until a workable plan for an international community of interests has been developed, a plan that will support such a peace, we must remain strong. America must be ready.

3

The Case against the
Federal Loyalty Program

✤ By Thurman Arnold [*]

THE fame and influence which the congressional
Committee on Un-American Activities has acquired by
investigating and publicizing those private opinions and
associations of American citizens of which it disapproves
is without precedent in our generation. With the aid of
a favorable press the committee has been able to force a
great industry, the motion picture producers, to agree to
discharge any employee who does not meet the vague
and nebulous standards of Americanism which the committee attempts to lay down. It has been able to coerce
the Truman administration to institute a series of investigations concerning the opinions and associations
of millions of government employees which have cost
between ten and twenty million dollars. Millions of
secret dossiers have been collected on almost all persons
in government, disclosing who are their friends, what
they think about political questions, what they said at
cocktail parties, with whom they associated at college,

---

[*] Judge Thurman Arnold, sometime Professor of Law, Yale
University, author, *The Folklore of Capitalism* and other books,
Assistant Attorney General, and Associate Justice of the U.S.
Court of Appeals, is now senior partner of the Washington law
firm of Arnold, Fortas and Porter, which has defended several
dozen persons faced with dismissal from federal employment
under the loyalty program.

and all the organizations they have ever joined. An elaborate system of inquisitorial and appellate tribunals has been set up with power to convict federal employees of disloyalty on evidence which is never disclosed to them. These special courts and this alien sort of procedure have been hitherto unknown in our history. A so-called loyalty program has become the center of a whirlwind of press and radio comment sweeping over the country and making all persons of dissenting views run for their cyclone cellars. I have been assigned the task of explaining the part that such a loyalty program can play in strengthening American political institutions.

In undertaking that assignment it may serve a useful purpose to examine why this program is popular, why so many people think it necessary for the protection of our democracy. We have been brought up to believe that freedom of speech and association is the cornerstone of democracy. We have hitherto thought that any organized government inquisition into the opinions and associations of anyone is contrary to the principle of freedom of speech. We have believed that it is a fundamental principle of justice that no man can be convicted of anything or censured or denounced by any kind of a government tribunal unless he is confronted with the evidence against him. We have believed this because we know that if an accused person can be convicted or censured on secret evidence, it follows that he can be convicted on no evidence. The loyalty program flies in the face of every one of these cherished traditions.

What then is the present peril to our political institutions which requires inquisitorial procedures of a character heretofore alien to our democracy?

The best, the most complete, and the most succinct explanation is offered by the Committee on Un-American Activities itself in a recent report. There are in this country, says the committee, about 74,000 members of the Communist Party. This malicious group is conniving by day and by night with the aim of eventually destroying our system of free enterprise and taking over our government agencies in the interests of the Soviet Republic. To a superficial observer this would seem, in a country of 150,000,000 people, an insignificant group for such a Herculean task. It might also be suggested that our so-called capitalistic institutions must be weak indeed if such a tiny minority can destroy them by infiltration and persuasion. But the committee has, what seems to it, an adequate answer. It appears that each one of the 74,000 Communists has ten friends, hostile to our system of government, ready to spring into action whenever the time is ripe. That means that there are nearly a million desperate and dangerous characters located in all walks of life, particularly in the government, willing to risk their careers, their persons, and their property to destroy America in the event of an armed conflict with Russia.

For those who believe this neither laws nor the judicial procedures which have protected us in the past seem adequate to meet this new threat from within. The membership of the Communist Party is secret. The nature of their poisonous activity requires that we not only root out Communists but all friends and associates of Communists. Indeed, to be really safe we must go further. We must root out the people whose attitudes and opinions indicate that they are weak enough to succumb to the blandishments of Communists and thus come under their influence. The fact that such people are inconsequential or that the government agencies with which they are connected have nothing to do with our foreign policy or our defense should not impair the thoroughness of our inquisition into the opinions and associations of government employees. We used to believe that it was better that ten guilty men escape than one innocent man be convicted. That principle must now be reversed. People of wavering faith in our Constitution or in our system of free enterprise are a constant and eternal menace. They must be purged.

If such people assert that their own freedom of opinion is impaired the answer is plain. The Soviets do not believe in freedom of speech. Why therefore should persons leaning toward that philosophy be accorded such a privilege? The Soviets do not accord due process of law in their investigations of persons suspected of disloyalty, so why should persons suspected of disloyalty to us be accorded due process? Such American privileges should be restricted to those Americans whose unwavering belief in American institutions is so firm that they cannot even be suspected of disloyalty to our institutions. This, I believe, is a fair statement of the principles which have guided the House Committee on Un-American Activities and which have been applauded by the press and the commentators who support the committee.

How these principles have been applied and interpreted is illustrated by the committee hearing investigating subversive influence in the motion picture industry. The following testimony of Jack Warner, high executive of a leading motion picture producing company, is typical:

Here at Warner Bros. we have no room for backslid Americans and wishy-washy concepts of Americanism.

We are happy that other motion-picture producers are joining in the aggressive course Warner Brothers has pioneered, and we hope still others will follow. . . .

The backsliders, the in-betweeners, and the straddlers are too content to drift with the dangerous tides the subversive elements are stirring. . . .

Anyone whom I thought was a Communist, or read in the papers that he was, was dismissed at the expiration of his contract. . . .

Ideological termites have burrowed into many American industries, organizations, and societies. *Wherever they may be, I say let us dig them out and get rid of them. My brothers and I will be happy to subscribe generously to a pest-removal fund.* We are willing to establish such a fund to ship to Russia the people who don't like our American system of government and prefer the communistic system to ours. [Emphasis supplied].

That's how strongly we feel about the subversives who want to overthrow our free American system.

.　　.　　.　　.　　.　　.　　.　　.　　.

Mr. Warner: When I say these people are Communists, as I said before, it is from hearsay. It was from printed forms I read in the Hollywood Reporter.

Mr. Thomas: But you got enough information to let them go?

Mr. Warner: I could tell in their writings and method of presentation of screen plays.

Mr. Stripling: You mean not calling them Communists?

Mr. Warner: They were un-American.

Mr. Stripling: For one reason or another you objected to the lines they were attempting to put in your scripts?

Mr. Warner: Yes.

Mr. Stripling: And you let these six people go. Can you name the six?

Mr. Warner: Yes, I think I can. I wish you would bear with me.

Of course, the application of these principles is not easy because of the sly and secretive way in which the Communists disseminate their deadly poison. Probably few Americans were even aware that American screen plays contained any Communist propaganda at all. It took Adolph Menjou who is not only a great actor but also, according to his sworn testimony, one of the most thorough students of Communism now at large to expose insidious Communistic infiltration into the movies. He testified before the committee in part as follows:

Mr. Stripling: Based upon your study, have you observed any Communist activity in the motion picture industry or in Hollywood, as we commonly refer to it?

Mr. Menjou: I would like to get the terminologies completely straight. Communistic activities—I would rather phrase it un-American or subversive, antifree enterprise, anticapitalistic. I have seen—pardon me.

Mr. Stripling: Have you observed any Communist propaganda in pictures, *or un-American propaganda* in pictures which were produced in Hollywood?

Mr. Menjou: I have seen no Communistic propaganda in pictures—if you mean "vote for Stalin," or that type of Communistic propaganda. I don't think that the Communists are stupid enough to try it that way. I have seen in certain pictures things I didn't think should have been in the pictures.

Mr. Stripling: Could you tell the committee whether or not there has been an effort on the part of any particular group in the motion-picture industry to inject Communist propaganda into pictures or to leave out scenes or parts of stories which would serve the Communist Party line?

Mr. Menjou: I don't like that term "Communist propaganda," because I have seen no such thing as Communist propaganda, such as *waving the hammer and sickle* in motion pictures. I have seen things that I thought were against what I consider good Americanism, in my feeling. I have seen pictures I thought shouldn't have been made—shouldn't have been made, let me put it that way [Emphasis supplied].

The enthusiasm of the committee for this clear statement of a national danger was evident from the remark of Mr. McDowell, one of its members, when Mr. Menjou concluded. Mr. McDowell said: "Mr. Menjou, I believe I told you last May on the west coast, that of all the thousands of people I have discussed Communism with you have the most profound knowledge of the background of communism I have ever met. . . . Mr. Chairman, in addition to being a great American, here is one of the greatest American patriots I have ever met."

Inspired by such testimony the motion picture industry, at the instigation of the Un-American Affairs Committee, took prompt action to save America. On November 27, 1947, every principal motion picture producer and all of the motion picture associations were represented at a meeting held in the Waldorf Astoria Hotel in New York City. There they entered into a solemn contract, each producer surrendering his own independence of action to the group, that no producer could continue the employment of any one who belonged to any group, whether Communist or not, which advocated the overthrow of the government "by illegal or unconstitutional method." They thus were careful to make their resolution broad enough to cover any reform measure which anyone anywhere could regard as unconstitutional. There was no indication of how charges of guilt by association or opinion were to be heard or resolved against the accused.

Having thus effectively curbed subversive influences in the motion picture industry the committee turned its attention to the government of the United States, which had been heretofore blind to our national peril. Under the prodding of the committee the administration finally woke up and established its present loyalty program. The government did not assert that there were many subversive persons in its ranks; however, it admitted that there were a few and that in order to rule out these few the opinions and associations of millions have to be investigated. This inquisitorial task was delegated to the FBI which was given an appropriation of over fifteen million dollars for that purpose.

At the outset it was realized that in conducting a loyalty program our traditional principle that every person accused must be confronted with the evidence against him must be dispensed with. This can be illustrated by an experience of my own in connection with one of these investigations. A courteous and efficient FBI agent came to my office. After identifying himself he asked whether I knew Mr. X. I replied that I did. He then told me that in 1940 Mr. X had joined the Washington Book Shop, a co-operative venture in book selling which has been denounced by the attorney general as under Communist domination. He then inquired whether I thought that my friend Mr. X had joined the bookshop simply to get books or whether this indicated a weakness of faith and susceptibility to subversive ideas. I asked if my answer would be disclosed to Mr. X and was assured it would not. This left me free to go to the limit with respect to Mr. X without fear of reprisal or embarrassment. It is obvious that had I thought that Mr. X would be confronted with my testimony I might have been under some restraint, and the investigation would thus have been hampered.

Records so collected are submitted to the department which employs the person investigated. It then becomes the responsibility of that department to hold a trial of any individuals whose dossiers appear to require further proceedings. Any person so tried is of course entitled to charges, but the charges cannot be so specific as to disclose the source of the information against him. They are therefore in very general terms, of which the following is a typical example: "You are charged with having associated with Communists or with persons or organizations in sympathy with Communism." In one case a government employee who was confronted with a charge like the above asked the loyalty board to specify what he had been accused of doing to enable him to prepare his defense. The board replied:

[63]

Well, we realize the difficulty you are in, in this position; on the other hand, I'd suggest that you might think back over your own career and perhaps in your own mind delve into some of the factors that have gone into your career which you think might have been subject to question and see what they are and see whether you'd like to explain or make any statement with regard to any of them. . . .

The loyalty boards are usually in the same difficulty as the accused in identifying the accusers of a government employee. For example, in one hearing the FBI had designated its informants to the board by symbols T1, T2, etc. At the hearing the following colloquy took place:

Q: Did you ever act as an organizer for the Communist Party or attempt to recruit others?

A: No.

Q: [It] has been corroborated, checked and verified. . . .

Attorney for employee: By whom?

A: I can't tell you. . . . We don't even know who the accuser is.

In another case the chairman replied to questions asking whether the informers against the accused were sworn as follows: "I don't think so. . . . I haven't the slightest knowledge as to who they were."

This is the process. Its defenders assert that there is no other way to conduct these hearings because if the accused knew anything about the sources of the information against him the information would dry up. Anyway, they say, no one has a right to a government job, and these trials are not like convictions for crimes.

Unfortunately it so happens that a discharge for disloyalty to one's government is worse than conviction for most crimes. It destroys the career of the accused and forever brands him as a quasi traitor.

Most of the persons who are tried are cleared, but the terror and anxiety of everyone under investigation is quite understandable in view of the terrible consequences of a discharge on loyalty grounds. As an example of this I cite one of the cases which our office handled. A young woman sought my aid who was under investigation for sympathizing with Communists. She was an assistant librarian at a salary of something over three thousand dollars in a government agency which had about as much to do with foreign policy or national defense as it had with seal hunting among the Eskimos. It was necessary to review her entire past life and all her associations. She was compelled to write out her political and economic views on practically everything. She had been an advanced New Dealer; she had some Negro friends. Once, in another department, she had protested violently that she did not want to see another war started and that she was against dropping atomic bombs on Russia. Her immediate boss had become angry and called her a Communist. She had been acquainted with another government employee who had been discharged. She was eventually cleared after a period of intense anxiety. Were these the things they were investigating, or was it something else? No one could find out. She had been engaged to a young man in another government department but insisted on postponing her marriage, fearing that because had she not been cleared it would have seriously interfered with his career.

When the case was over she asked how she might avoid such anxiety in the future. I told her that there was only one way. She had better drop her Negro friends because such acquaintanceships are not usual, and it is wise to conform to a regular pattern. It would be wise for her to express no views whatever on any programs which are not generally accepted as conservative. Independence of thought and action today, I told her, is a hazard for any government employee. There is of course not much chance of the lightning striking you again, but you never can tell. Nobody knows what gossip is in your file, and nobody can find out. I know of one government employee who was investigated three separate times although he was cleared each time.

The difficulty, of course, is that the government loyalty hearings seek to determine whether there is "a reasonable doubt of loyalty" of the employee. Loyalty is a loose word. To many people membership in a consumer's co-operative indicates disloyalty to American principles. In one case a member of the board sitting on the loyalty of an employee asked whether the employee thought it was proper to mix white and Negro plasma, an opinion he seemed to think of significance in determining loyalty.

The loyalty program assumes that everyone should know how far he can go in his thinking without being disloyal to the principles of Americanism. Of course, this is an impossible thing for anyone to determine. It all depends on the bias and attitude of some loyalty board. If you want to be safe, you had better stick to the philosophy of that great actor and expert on Communism, Adolph Menjou, whose views we have quoted elsewhere in this article. As proof of this I cite the following questions which have been asked in various hearings and which are unfortunately typical:

What do you think of the loyalty order?

What do you think of the new conscription program? Are you in favor of it?

Are you in favor of the Marshall Plan?

There is a suspicion in the record that you are in sympathy with the underprivileged. Is this true?

It is of the utmost importance, of course, that the books which employees read be carefully supervised and investigated, as appears from the following testimony taken from five different hearings:

HEARING No. 1

Q: What type of books did your associates have?

A: They had all kinds, popular novels, a general assortment.

Q: Any social, political economy?

A: I don't remember seeing any.

Q: Did you ever discuss with your associates their taste in the literature that they had?

A: Yes, we had discussions.

Q: Explain to the Board the extent of your association in this respect. . . .

Q: What kind of books, by title, did you purchase, what kind of literature?

HEARING No. 2

Q: When you went to X's apartment did you observe any books she had in the apartment?

A: There was a small book case.

Q: How many copies of Howard Fast's novels have you read?

A: One.

Q: Do you know the name of it?

A: Freedom Road.

Q: Much impressed with it?

HEARING No. 3

Q: Do you think the Russian form of government is good for the Russians?

A: I don't know.

HEARING No. 4

Q: Did the books in X's home appear to have been purchased from bookclubs or individually from bookstores?

HEARING No. 5

Q: Did you ever hear any political discussions at X's home?

Q: Did you ever attend any political forums at X's home?

Q: Are your friends and associates intelligent, clever?

There is now pending in the United States District Court for the District of Columbia a case which we hope will eventually reach the Supreme Court. It is the case of Dorothy Bailey, who was a supervisor of the United States Employment Service training section, a job of responsibility requiring expert skill. She had had long service in the government since 1933. Her record was consistently good, and her efficiency ratings were uniformly high. Indeed, she was recognized throughout the country as an expert in her field. The principal charge against her was that she had been a member of the Communist Party or else in close association with it. The question before the board which heard her case was, as the board stated, whether there were reasonable grounds for belief that she was disloyal to the government.

She denied the charges, and a long hearing was held. The record contains no evidence whatever against her. On the contrary, it contains an enormous amount of affirmative evidence in her favor, including affidavits as to her character by many prominent and conservative people. She never followed what has been called the party line.

The sole case against her was a statement by the board that information had been supplied to it that she had been a member of the Communist Party and had engaged in various other activities which cast doubt upon her loyalty. Neither she nor her counsel was able to find out what that information was, or who had supplied it to the board. She was convicted of disloyalty. Her name was released to the papers. She appealed. This time another record was made which again contained no derogatory evidence whatever. Her conviction was upheld, and again this was released to the papers. She is branded as a quasi traitor. She cannot again work for the government, and the stigma of her conviction prevents her pursuing her career in private life. A penitentiary sentence could not more effectively destroy her reputation and her opportunity for a livelihood. This punishment has been meted out on secret information which the government refuses to disclose.

[69]

It is obvious to anyone that if a person can be convicted on secret evidence he can be convicted on no evidence. We say that this conviction violates every American concept of due process and all our traditions of a fair trial.

The answer made by defenders of the process is that no one has a right to a government job and that a government job is all that Dorothy Bailey has lost. This, we submit, is absurd. She has been given drastic punishment and deprived of all the protections which our Constitution is supposed to give. That, stated in nontechnical terms, is the issue which will be before the court in the Dorothy Bailey case.

My function in this article is not to discuss the law but rather the effect of the loyalty program conducted in the way I have described in strengthening American political institutions. The central idea of that program is that drastic punishment may be inflicted on an individual because he has violated standards of belief and opinion so vague as to be impossible of definition. The evidence on which such convictions may be had is such that it would stand up in no American court. This process is one which we associate with Soviet Russia, not with America. The answer, therefore, is that with our loyalty program we are destroying rather than strengthening American political institutions and ideals.

Spy hunts and heresy hunts are not unknown in America. They are products of fear and hysteria. But this is the first time in our generation that a quasi-judicial process has been prostituted to give the trappings of legitimacy to such activities.

What is the peril that confronts us? As President

Roosevelt said in his first inaugural address, the only thing we need to fear, in assuming the responsibilities of world leadership forced upon us by these revolutionary times, is fear itself. Is it possible that a small group of Communists by infiltration and persuasion can destroy our political and economic institutions and induce us to accept their culture? Of course it isn't. Never in the history of the world has any foreign government ever been able to change the culture and the ideals of another nation by propaganda or persuasion. As we are learning today in Japan and Germany, this is almost an impossible task, even in countries which we occupy. Our danger does not come from the Communists but from ourselves. Our real peril is the committees and the loyalty boards which are instilling lack of confidence in the stability of American institutions. These boards have gone far in destroying independence of thought among those who are responsible for our foreign and domestic policy. At the very least they have made independent thinking dangerous. Only a confident America can assume world leadership in the twentieth century. We cannot impress on other nations the idea of the sacredness of individual independence while we are intent on destroying it at home.

Communism is never a result of foreign persuasion. It comes from internal discontent. Every revolutionary movement the world has ever known arose out of internal economic maladjustments. All of them were inspired by the ancient revolutionary philosophy of taking away from the few and giving to the many under rigid state control. Such movements are not defeated but are actually encouraged by attempting to suppress the ideas by which they are inspired. America is a country where the founding fathers knew this obvious truth and framed a constitution on this principle. Today under the influence of the loyalty program we are beginning to doubt that great tradition.

A long time ago Philip of Spain and Elizabeth of England were engaged in a cold war. Elizabeth was employing against Spain all the tactics of intrigue and deceit that Soviet Russia is now employing against us. She was capturing Spanish cargoes by secretly commissioning men like Drake and Hawkins while publicly denying her responsibility for this privateering. Spain was Catholic. Elizabeth was Protestant. To the Catholics of that day the Protestants were like our present Communists. By intrigue, infiltration, and persuasion they were trying to undermine that cornerstone of the Spanish government, the Catholic Church. And so Philip thought that the danger was that Catholic Spain might succumb to the blandishments of heresy. To meet that peril he called on the Spanish Inquisition. Every time Elizabeth's privateers sank a Spanish ship or sacked a Spanish town in the New World more heretics were investigated. Did this strengthen the institutions of Spain? We know the answer today. It bled Spain white. It destroyed the initiative and independence of her best individuals. The Armada failed because it was headed by pious but incompetent men.

We have done similar things in America. The Puritan theocracy thought that the Quakers were insidiously preaching a doctrine which might destroy the foundations of its theocratic government. And so it passed savage legislation harrying the Quakers out of the land.

Did this strengthen the theocracy? The answer is that it lost for Massachusetts its charter.

The Communists in America today are not making America Communistic. Instead they are driving it into bitter hatred of Communism. They are making it unsafe to join any organization dedicated to economic or political reform. They destroyed any chance which Henry Wallace may have had to defeat President Truman. They are assisting conservative thought, not destroying it. They present about the same amount of internal danger to America's political institutions as the cult of nudists does to the clothing industry.

Only in one respect are they hurting us, and that is to the extent that they induce us to lose faith in democratic institutions and traditions. We are fighting a cold war. In such times, above all, we need faith in the strength of our way of life and our traditions of individual freedom of opinion and association.

Are we getting a more realistic understanding today of how to handle the cold war with Russia through the un-American loyalty hunts we are now conducting? The Russian Revolution, like the French Revolution, is a historical event. To put the question, as many loyalty boards do, as to whether or not the Russian Revolution is a good thing or a bad thing is like asking whether the French Revolution was a good or a bad thing. All such questions can do is to show the unrealistic attitude in the appraisal of historical events which the loyalty boards are seeking to impose upon American citizens.

Dorothy Bailey is the first individual in our generation convicted by a government tribunal solely on the basis of secret information given to the court, which tried her by secret police and secret paid informers. All she was permitted to know was that somewhere in some secret file such information had been collected. She could not find out what the information was or who gave it to the court. She stands branded today as disloyal to her country. She can obtain neither government nor private employment. Her career, which took half a lifetime to build up, is gone. The case is before the court for their judgment.

It is my hope and my belief that this case, or some other like it, may wake up America to the realization that not in this way can it find either security in peace or strength in war.

Additional Thoughts on the Federal Loyalty Program

BY ARTHUR E. SUTHERLAND, Jr.[*]

GOVERNMENT is a complex business that increases in amount and complexity as the world becomes more crowded. Inevitably it interferes more and more with the individual's convenience. The greatest problem of national govenment is to reconcile crowding with decency, to maintain an intricate organization while annoying the individual as little as possible. No simple,

---

[*] Professor Arthur E. Sutherland, Jr., of the Cornell University Law School was asked to append his brief postscript to Judge Arnold's article, not as a rebuttal but as a reminder that there is a problem of security.

sweeping measure can accomplish this reconciliation, only the endless compromises, adjustments, persuasions which so irritate the newcomer in the field. There is little free wild territory left for colonizing. Crowding generations similarly affect international ambitions. An expanding technology is exhausting essential materials. There is world-wide competition for allegiance, propaganda on a vast scale, electioneering for continents; and along with the bidding for allegiance goes the threat of war.

Policing against international disorder is not fundamentally different from the internal variety; in both cases the citizen is apt to be irked. In the latter, he may make speeches about "eliminating all this bureaucracy that is controlling our lives," but, if he thinks, he realizes that no such simple solution is possible. Judge Arnold seems to suggest a similarly simple, and similarly inadmissible, remedy for irksome loyalty procedures. He would eliminate them. "Our danger," he says, "does not come from the Communists but from ourselves. Our real peril is the committees and the loyalty boards which are instilling lack of confidence in the stability of American institutions." Like most discussions of governmental theory, this one soon reduces itself to opposing statements of belief. If, after making due allowance for the rhetorical device of exaggeration, one may still suppose Judge Arnold to believe that many Americans are losing confidence in the stability of their institutions, I can only say that I believe that he is wrong.

This discussion concerns President Truman's Executive Order No. 9835, of March 21, 1947, and the means taken to enforce it. Essentially the order directs that the

United States, through "loyalty boards," determine whether federal employees are disloyal—because they seek to change the form of government of the United States by unconstitutional means, or because they serve the interests of another government in preference to our own. Customarily in discussions of the subject this is the point at which objection is made that loyalty and security are being confused; that security measures are understandable and proper; but that security among federal employees is fundamentally different from loyalty. Security is jeopardized not only by enemy sympathies but by the drunken or the loquacious, one is told; loyalty is different. This I am unable to follow. Granted that the bibulous and the garrulous are out of place where they have access to secrets of state; why does this indicate that one who, put to the choice, would prefer to serve a potential enemy rather than his own country, should continue in the employ of the United States?

Judge Arnold points out that the Loyalty Order affects, among others, minor government employees who have no access to important secrets; and that in certain cases the procedures of some Loyalty Boards have been unjust, and that members have sometimes confused zeal for innocent domestic reform with treachery to the United States. For purposes of discussion one could concede both points, without admitting that wholehearted devotion to the United States on the part of its servants is not a suitable subject of public concern.

A reasonable argument could be made to the effect that the Loyalty Order, insofar as it applies to, say, laborers on government construction or others having no access to sensitive spots, is more trouble than it is worth. Surely no argument is needed to convince any reasonable person that government procedures to determine loyalty or its lack should be as completely fair, as scrupulous of the rights of the respondent, as man can devise. The sanction of public scorn for the disloyal is too complete and too devastating to permit any less tenderness for the citizen's reputation. Eloquent and sincerely felt criticisms, such as those made by Judge Arnold, serve an important purpose when they draw attention to injustices, even if sporadic and infrequent. Certainly no reasonable Loyalty Board can be permitted to find disaffection solely from a zeal for domestic reform. If so, various national and state administrations and legislatures are in danger of like accusation! Redevelopment housing in Chicago or New York has no connection with Russian aims in the Balkans; and any confusion on this subject in the minds of federal functionaries or lay reformers needs clearing up. To the extent that Judge Arnold helps do so, he earns our thanks.

But the difficulty is that he would throw out the baby with the bath. A man can be heartily in favor of fair play by federal judicial and quasi-judicial bodies without agreeing that the only way to achieve this is to drop all consideration of loyalty among federal functionaries. "Is it possible," says Judge Arnold, "that a small group of Communists by infiltration and persuasion can destroy our political and economic institutions and induce us to accept their culture? Of course it isn't." One can agree heartily with this, despite the contrary experience of Czechoslovakia. Lincoln was right when he said you can't fool all Americans very long. But is the probable unsuccess of sly enemies a reason for leaving them in office as our servants? Must we choose between being unjust or being gullible? This seems a statement of defeatism. No one suggests abolishing police because they are sometimes stupid or brutal; the remedy is to improve the police. So here it should be possible to achieve one more satisfactory compromise between individual immunity from undue harassment, and undue license to the public enemy. This is not simple, to be sure, but government in the mid-twentieth century is as complicated as it is inevitable.

4

The Presidency:
Its Burden and Its Promise

❧ By Don K. Price[*]

THE White House, the storm center of American politics, has for a half-century had more continuity in its top civil service staff than any other part of the executive branch. The increase in the work of that staff illustrates what has happened, since McKinley's administration made America a world power, to the Presidency of the United States. Ira Smith, for example, came to the White House under McKinley and left under Truman. He received the President's mail. Calvin Coolidge used to come down and sit on the corner of Ira's desk while Ira personally slit the envelopes and passed him his letters. But before Ira Smith retired in 1948, after fifty-one years of service, he headed a considerable organization that handled more mail than the post office of many a small city, and he had had to move out of the White House into the old State-War-Navy building that now houses the Executive Office of the President.

Now we might take the statistics on the mail received by Ira Smith, or those on government expenditures, or

[*] Don K. Price, Associate Director of the Public Administration Clearing House, was the assistant to former President Hoover on his study of the Presidency for the Hoover Commission, and helped prepare the Commission's report on the *General Management of the Executive Branch,* especially its recommendations on the Executive Office of the President.

[81]

those on civil service employees in the executive branch as indications of the growth in the burden on the American Presidency during the past half-century. But it is important not to look on the administrative problems of the Presidency as if they were problems of office management and nothing more, or even as problems that arise mainly out of the quantity of business to be handled.

The main administrative problems of the Presidency have not arisen from sheer quantity or from the size of the executive branch. They have arisen because the United States, during much of the nineteenth century and several decades of the twentieth, complicated the President's job by weakening his administrative authority and his ability to hold his subordinates accountable. Today the state of the nation and of world affairs requires a more closely knit executive branch than we have had for more than a century. We have a chronic budgetary deficit, and only tighter administrative discipline can save money. More important, only a sensitive and responsive kind of teamwork among the top officials of the executive branch can enable the President to be an effective national leader in a time that demands effective leadership for the strengthening of free institutions all over the world.

Personal leadership is important, but personal leadership is not enough. The Presidency is an institution. As an institution, it is probably America's greatest contribution to the art or science of government. And if it is to be reformed and strengthened, its improvements must be in harmony with the rest of our constitutional system.

Someone has remarked that a country is never without

honor save among its own prophets. Many of our students of government have been so alert to various difficulties in our constitutional system that they have not appreciated the peculiar advantages of the Presidency and the way in which its problems—even its routine managerial problems—are linked with essential features of our constitutional and political system.

The Federalists who put the Constitution into effect were keenly aware, week by week, that they were setting precedents that would determine the patterns of American government for a long time to come. The basic principles that the Federalists built into the Presidency still determine today the main lines along which it may be strengthened as an institution.

Three of these principles deserve particular attention.

First, the direct responsibility of the President to the people is the best guarantee of the independence of the Congress and thus the most effective protection for our system of federalism.

The Constitutional Convention knew that if the Congress were to constitute the executive, or share in the responsibility for supervising it, the results would be not that the Congress would have greater control over the executive but exactly the opposite. A few decades later, by letting party conventions take over from the congressional caucus the job of nominating Presidents, the Congress kept its legislative machinery independent of the great contest for political power in the United States —the election of the President. And because the Congress and the President can be mutually independent in their tenure of office, it was only the Electoral College, in the United States, that was reduced to a rubber stamp

[83]

by the rise of democratic political parties. In Great
Britain it was the Parliament.

The Federalists wanted Congress to be independent
for a purpose—as a permanent guarantee of our federalism.

Their foresight was remarkable. As our society and
technology have become more centralized decade by
decade, the legalistic defenses of states' rights have become weaker and weaker. But the states themselves have
become stronger and stronger, so that they have not only
greatly expanded their own functions but have insisted
on administering large parts of the programs initiated
and paid for by the federal government, which the federal government might easily have administered for
itself. And their claim for a share in the national administration is effectively supported by the Congress, the
members of which are not tempted, by having a share
in executive authority, to seek to extend federal operations at the expense of the states. Even some of the best
students of federalism from other countries still think
that the role of our states is defended mainly by the
Constitution and the courts—and so, for example, they
fail to understand how the states, having once turned
over the employment services to the federal government,
were able in spite of the President to take them back
again.

An equally important issue today is one that the
Federalists could not have foreseen in its present form:
how much freedom should be left to private business
corporations? Just as in the modern world the affairs of
national and state governments are inevitably intertwined, so that the state governments cannot defend

their independence at any legalistic barricade, so also the affairs of the great corporations are intertwined with those of government. They, too, must ultimately defend their independence, or rather their partial independence, on the grounds of their utility to the people—not behind any constitutional barrier. And the judge of their claims to freedom is no longer the courts but the Congress, whose members are not responsible for executive programs and can therefore consider the role of private institutions and their relation to the state from a position of relative detachment.

As a result, while other countries—even other democracies—see national ownership as the only way to bring the basic industries into a proper relation with the public interest, we are experimenting with a wide range of devices, ranging from outright ownership to limited regulation. The device that most conspicuously fails to fit into our old patterns of thinking about government and private business is the device of administration by contract. In the Atomic Energy Commission's program, for example, twelve out of every thirteen of the employees involved are working, not for the government, but for private companies or institutions that have contracts with the government and thus carry out government policy. Federal steamboat inspection was started early in the nineteenth century, and to this day every ocean vessel and every merchant sailor must pass examination by a federal inspector. But the twentieth-century form of transportation—the airplane and its pilot—is inspected mainly by private companies under contract with the Civil Aeronautics Administration and working under its standards.

Our economists have been inclined to believe that our governmental institutions are shaped by the nature of our economic ones. But it seems to me that the contrary is true—or is also true. For while other countries are nationalizing their industries as fast as dominant legislatures see the connection between industry and national policy or national security, we in the United States are creating a kind of economic federalism. This is a system in which business corporations retain a high degree of independence even while playing an integral part in public administration. Like our political federalism, it is kept in a state of balance by the fact that the mutual independence of the executive and legislative branches keeps either from wishing to extend too greatly the economic authority of the other.

In short, the first important fact about the Presidency is that it was set up on a basis of co-ordinate authority with the Congress in order to avoid the creation of unlimited central power. And this separation of powers now, long after most of the specific legalistic barriers have become obsolete, is a strong political protection not only for the states and local governments but for private institutions as well.

The second point is that, while the Federalists used the Presidency to make a dynasty unnecessary, the Jacksonians used it to prevent the growth of a bureaucracy.

The spoils system was no better than a system of public plunder, and the merit system which has generally displaced it was an essential step in the interest of both administrative efficiency and public morality. But as we adopted the merit system we kept—at least by comparison with most European governments—a kind of limited rotation in office. More administrators and scientists move back and forth between the typical federal department and the private group with which it is related than between it and other government departments. I suppose, without counting them, that for every scientist or administrator in the Department of Agriculture who has worked in some other federal department, there are a half-dozen who have worked for a land grant college or a state agricultural agency.

The United States could never have tolerated this system if it had had to depend on its career officials for continuity and stability.

In a parliamentary system, the top administrators of all departments must almost necessarily, if the nation is to avoid great confusion, be a single permanent career corps. No matter how stable the government, there is always the constitutional possibility of a change at any time, and no country could afford to face the danger of changes in the top civil service with each change in the ministry. And in this respect, the top civil service could cause political instability as well as suffer from its results. If civil servants, by moving back and forth between government and private life, were to acquire political connections of their own, it would be impossible to keep the civil service itself from being the subject of partisan attack in the parliament and perhaps the cause of continual cabinet crises.

As the British Association of First Division Civil Servants puts it, the top civil service must "set . . . wider and more enduring considerations against the exigencies of the moment, in order that the parliamentary convenience of today may not become the parliamentary embarrassment of tomorrow. . . ." Moreover, "The Civil Servant has to act so as not to embarrass his Minister and the Government of the Day in their relations with Parliament and with organizations having political power." [1]

In the United States, on the contrary, continuity and stability do not come from the civil service. They come rather from the direct election and the fixed term of office of the President. And, in another sense, they come from the legislative branch, where well-seasoned committee leaders, supported by the seniority rule and accustomed to decades of bipartisan collaboration, put the brakes on the impetuous leadership of each new wave of hopeful administrators brought in by the President to help bring about changes in policy.

It is not only true that our public administrators, as individuals, are not a class apart from the rest of society, with separate views and interests. Some of our executive bureaus or agencies themselves take on some of the characteristics of private corporations. They have traditionally been chartered—or rather, established—by act of Congress; their administrators have little in common with those of other departments; and with the support of private pressure groups and friendly congressional committees they can sit tight and follow their own policies regardless of the President. I think it is safe to say that the Army Corps of Engineers is far less respon-

---

[1] Royal Commission on the Civil Service (1929–1930), Appendix VIII to Minutes of Evidence: Statement Submitted by the Association of First Division Civil Servants (London: H.M. Stationery Office, 1930).

sive than many a great private corporation to the general policy of the President.

The United States invented the Presidency to keep from getting a king. And because of the presidential system, and the continuity and stability it affords, the United States does not need a closed bureaucracy and never has had one.

The third great point about the Presidency that determines the way in which that office must be organized and administered is that it was set up so that it would not have to be supported by either a single political party or an established church.

Everybody remembers President Washington's naïve notion that he could get along without being the head of a party. Everyone knows that the President now has to be head of a party. Everyone agrees that each of our two parties in the Congress ought to have a greater degree of discipline and responsibility than it now has. But it is still necessary to remember that loyalty to a party may come into conflict with loyalty to the nation. We are inclined to forget that the only time we ever permitted a partisan difference to coincide with a fundamental difference in political principles and economic interests we had a civil war. And the Civil War persisted for a half-century or longer in the form of bureaucratic bushwhacking, or the putting of party patronage (in jobs or tariffs) ahead of government in the public interest.

It is easy to forget this point, although the memory of it is rooted in some of the more archaic procedures of the Congress, which are designed to prevent, rather than encourage, the drawing of clear-cut party lines on issues of policy or principle. The civil war of the seventeenth century persuaded the British that they did not want a republican executive who would be responsible, like Cromwell, directly to the people—especially if he were backed by a politico-religious party. The Civil War of the nineteenth century made Americans a little nervous about drawing party lines so tight in the Congress as to make it impossible for regional and economic groups to form different alliances with respect to every important issue.

Someone should make a study to find out how much of our domestic as well as our foreign policy has genuinely bipartisan support. He would find, I suspect, that on more than nine-tenths of the items in the federal budget there is no clear party line on the policies involved, even though the two parties may differ on the amount of money to be spent.

It is, I believe, a pity that we carry this distrust of parties so far that, in addition to avoiding the creation of ideological parties, we destroy party discipline and party responsibility in the Congress. American liberals and American scholars, who joined forces in denouncing Cannonism, are to blame for making impossible the coordination of the congressional committees in the interest of a party program. But if we are to go off balance in either direction this is the safer one, for there is certainly no danger that in the present state of American politics we will see either the Republicans or the Democrats become the fanatical driving force of a single-party system.

Now these three aspects of the Presidency—how its independent status makes it possible for the Congress to maintain an independent check on the executive branch, how it makes unnecessary a closed career corps of administrators, and how it prevents clear-cut party lines from developing on policy issues—increase our ability to deal with each issue pragmatically and on its merits. That means that we have a better chance to let scientists, both natural and social scientists, bring their skills to bear on the solution of public issues in an objective spirit, and themselves move into positions of administrative influence.

It is important to make these general points for two reasons. First, if we understand them and consider them fundamental, we will avoid some of the superficially attractive reforms which are most frequently proposed for the Presidency. Second, it is essential to understand them in order to understand what should be done to improve the institution of the Presidency, for these general features are the fundamental pillars around which any improvements must be built.

Most of the ideas for reforming the Presidency that seem to me unworkable fail to take into account how slowly and painfully we have built up a partially unified national government, step by step, on a foundation of legislative and executive agreement. The main features of the presidential system which I have been discussing add up to a system of pluralism. But along with its great —and I believe overwhelming—advantages, this kind of political pluralism has corresponding defects. It is extremely difficult to build up a unified administration when every detail of organization and administration can be made into a political issue.

This is a difficult practical result of founding our government not on an inherited tradition (as is done in a constitutional monarchy, for example) but on a decision of the people. It leaves a constitutional ambiguity: the President is responsible for the administration of the executive branch, but the Congress may to any degree it likes determine the organization and procedures of the executive branch. It was this point that led John Adams to believe that the Constitution might prove unworkable because the President was not given an absolute veto by which to protect himself against legislative encroachment.

Walter Bagehot remarked that in the English Constitution there was first a dignified part which the people understood, and behind it was an efficient part by which the government was really operated. But when people begin setting up their governmental agencies by federal and state constitutions and municipal charters, they get in the habit of trying to make the dignified and efficient elements identical. As a result, the people both restrict executive authority and make a lot of inconsistent decisions. And so the unity and the discretionary authority which are necessary to any administrative organization are difficult to attain in the United States government, and they must be developed by painstaking nonpartisan agreement. Without such agreement it is impossible for our Congress to consider policies, which are determined best by general statutes and by the appropriation of funds, without being diverted by disputes over administration. It is much easier for the opponent of a policy to defeat it by making its administration unworkable than to get it voted down on its merits.

By contrast we see no such difficulties in the British government, which by its classical nineteenth-century example still exercises a fatal fascination over many of our political scientists, long after most of our economists have escaped the influence of nineteenth-century classical economics. While our legislature, through its independent committees, can and does bring out opposing views on policies by questioning civil servants at all levels of administration—and then freely amends any measure—the British government has a far more effective separation of powers.

Under this system His Majesty's civil service has taken on some of the constitutional characteristics of the Crown itself. It has the right to permanent tenure on condition that it stay out of any public disagreement over policies or politics. As the King can in legal theory do no wrong, since a minister must take responsibility for each of his acts, so the civil service cannot be held responsible, since only a minister can be called to account on a policy issue by the House of Commons.

If you read the proceedings of the most recent committees set up by the House of Commons to consider its procedure on public business, you will see that there are at least two ways in which the Parliament is not omnipotent. DeLolme remarked in admiration that the only thing it could not do was change a woman into a man, but it is quite clear that in the twentieth century, no matter how much some of its members might wish to do so, it cannot create a committee apart from the Cabinet to give independent consideration to policy issues. As a result the vote of no confidence is the only sanction by which the legislature can force the executive to change a policy decision, and this sanction is so drastic that it has become almost as obsolete as impeachment itself.

Yet it is on assumptions that are proper to this quite different constitutional system that we have based many of our most widely discussed ideas for the reform of the American executive.

One such idea includes various suggestions to increase the harmony of legislative-executive relations. The two proposals most widely discussed are either to have the President construct his Cabinet from a joint legislative council to be created by the two houses of Congress and to contain its leading members, or to have the heads of executive departments defend their policies in the Congress by answering questions on the floor of the Senate and the House. Consider the effect on the Presidency and on even our present degree of imperfect unity in the executive branch if each executive decision by the President were subject to the advice and consent —or even public discussion—by a congressional leadership which is under no binding obligations of party discipline, and which through independent committees can deal directly with the officials of subordinate bureaus and divisions.

We would run the grave risk of imitating the anarchy of the French parliamentary system rather than the tight discipline of the British, if we were to set up the kind of formal legislative-executive liaison that is frequently discussed, without giving the President the kind of control over the legislative process that is taken for granted by the British Prime Minister. Few would argue that the President could have the same discretion in promoting Congressmen to positions of legislative leadership that the Prime Minister exercises in picking his Cabinet, or the Prime Minister's authority over the legislative cal-

endar, or the privilege of preventing legislative committees from amending important policy measures, or
the right to dissolve the Congress if he failed to get the
support of a majority on any issue. But without the
reciprocal responsibility that would be provided by such
fundamental changes, by formalizing congressional su-
pervision over the administration of the executive branch
we would not only lessen the unity of our government
but make it less responsive to general public opinion.

Those who seek mainly to increase legislative-executive harmony leave out the most important element in
the situation—the electorate. It is an essential part of
American constitutional procedure to have a certain
amount of continuing disagreement between Congress
and the executive branch in order to bring policy issues
before the people. To increase the direction of executive
departments by congressional committees would settle
too many issues at lower levels before the President could
formulate them, generalize them into his over-all program, and bring them before the Congress as a whole,
and the people, for consideration.

The second misleading approach to reforming the
Presidency is based on a mistaken idea of the distinction
between policy and administration. This is the proposal
to relieve the President of his administrative burden by
entrusting authority over administration to a subordinate, leaving the President free (in theory) to decide
questions of policy.

It is not too far from the truth to say that in the British
government policy is what the Cabinet decides, and administration is what the civil servants then do about it.
There is no danger in making this useful though artificial

distinction because the government, with its full control over legislative procedures, can insist on having the administrative authority to carry out any policy decision. But this distinction cannot have the same meaning at all in the United States. If the policy is to combat inflation, that is only a general way of saying that perhaps a new post office may have to be denied to Kokomo, or a new levee to the Mississippi Delta, or that the Commodity Credit Corporation must pay less for surplus potatoes. And the President of the United States, no matter how much he may have support from the Congress as a whole on a general policy, may see it defeated because his department heads or bureau chiefs, in concert with congressional committees, beat him down on the details of that policy.

For this reason no American President has ever been willing to support a scheme which would, by any kind of formalized arrangement, give any subordinate executive officer too broad a control over the administrative aspects of government affairs. The most famous proposal of this kind in recent years, of course, was the idea widely discussed during 1948 that the Vice-President should be made the head of a Department of Administration, including what are now the Bureau of the Budget, the Civil Service Commission, the Public Buildings Administration, and other "housekeeping" agencies. Similar schemes proposed in 1948 to the Commission on Organization of the Executive Branch were to create such a department under a Cabinet officer appointed by the President, or to transfer the functions of fiscal and budgetary administration from the Presidency to the Treasury Department, a proposal that was argued partly in terms of a mistaken analogy with the British Treasury. A less pretentious proposal is that the President should have a civilian chief of staff, who would be the head of all his staff agencies.

It is especially hard in the United States to draw a clear line, at high levels, between the administrator and the politician, and it would be very hard indeed to persuade a President that a Chief of Administration would not develop definite ideas on policy objectives, or seek to promote his own public career, or attract the support of those who want to exploit any possible difference of opinion on policies between him and the President. It is not enough of a safeguard to say that the President would be free to remove such an officer. The removal of a major subordinate is a kind of political surgery that it is not easy for an administration to undergo. Moreover, the man who would be in charge of all the staff functions would be in a strategic position to define the issues and produce the expert evidence in such a way that the President, as an individual, would be nearly powerless to determine his own course of action or to decide the policy issues which he wished to bring up for public consideration in the light of his political strategy.

The Hoover Commission took none of these lines of approach. Instead it proposed to strengthen the Presidency clearly within the limits of the main principles of the presidential system—the existence of a legislature which is free to defend federalism and free institutions, of an executive branch with no closed career corps, and of a system of limited party responsibility without party division on ideological lines.[2]

The first of the basic principles which seemed to guide the Commission's recommendations was this: efficient and responsible management is more likely to result from a department head's full responsibility to the President than from all the detailed rules and regulations that can be applied by Congress and by the President's staff agencies.

The Commission pointed out that the constitutional authority of the President over the executive branch had been dissipated by the creation of a great many independent agencies and obstructed by the grant of various forms of statutory independence to bureaus and subdivisions of the executive departments. Hence it proposed that the executive branch should be organized into a smaller number of major departments and that the head of each should have a clearer responsibility for its management. It argued that, to fix such responsibility, the department head have authority to determine the internal organization of his department and to decide which of its subdivisions could most efficiently spend money appropriated to the department for any given purpose by the Congress.

This general recommendation was put in greater detail by proposals for changes in the budgetary, appropriations, and accounting structure, in the system of personnel recruitment and classification, and in the

---

[2] Needless to say, the following interpretation represents the personal views of the author, and not the official theory of the Commission or any of its members.

purchasing system, all in the direction of freeing the department head from many detailed restrictions and regulations, in order that he might have a chance to administer efficiently the programs for which he is responsible to the President and accountable to the Congress. These changes would free the executive departments from much of the detailed control now exercised by congressional committees, by the General Accounting Office, and by the central staff and service agencies of the executive branch—the Executive Office of the President as well as the Civil Service Commission, the Bureau of Federal Supply, and others.

The second general principle followed by the Commission was that the Congress, in order to concentrate its attention more clearly on the great issues of policy, should delegate more responsibility for reorganization to the President.

On policy issues there are enough conflicting pressures from conflicting interests in our society so that the Congress can cancel one out against the other and make a decision in the national interest. On any question of organization, however, the only actively interested group is the bureau in question, supported by its own clientele, which never wants to be held effectively responsible by the chief executive. Just as the President can be a successful executive only if he delegates a great deal of authority to his subordinates, so the Congress as a whole can control policies only if it keeps its committees from becoming obligated to the various bureaus —and it can do so only if it delegates a large measure of responsibility on questions of organization to the President. For this reason the Hoover Commission rec-

ommended that the Congress grant permanently to the
President the authority to initiate reorganization plans
under a procedure first suggested by President Hoover
in 1931, first enacted under President Roosevelt in 1939,
and re-enacted under President Truman in 1945. This is
a procedure in which the Congress gives the President
responsibility for reorganizing the executive branch not
by an outright delegation to take executive action (as it
has done from time to time in both war and peace), but
by inviting him to submit plans which will take effect
unless both Houses of the Congress vote, within a certain period, to reject them.

The third general principle embodied in the Hoover
Commission's recommendations was that the President,
in order to meet the responsibilities placed upon him by
the Constitution and the Congress, needs a strong Executive Office and full discretion in using it.

The need for staff services in an Executive Office is
partly a result of the President's constitutional duty to
see that the laws are faithfully executed. But it is also
the result of the demand by the Congress that the
President act as the principal legislative leader by pre-
senting a program for congressional consideration. In
addition to the Civil Service Act of 1883, which put on
the President the responsibility of issuing the Civil
Service rules, and the Budget and Accounting Act of
1921, which made him responsible for submitting an
executive budget, the Employment Act of 1946 requires
him to recommend a program for the stabilization of the
national economy. The three principal staff agencies
which the Hoover Commission unanimously recommended for the Executive Office are the agencies to help

the President carry out the duties placed on him by these three acts—a budget office, a personnel office, and an economic advisory office.

No person can carry the President's responsibilities single-handed. The very size and complexity of governmental administration put the President at the mercy of the Congress, for he cannot hire a single staff member to help him carry out his constitutional and legal responsibilities unless the Congress will appropriate funds for the purpose. The Congress has not been quick to realize the need for an adequate presidential staff. Until 1945 the White House Office had been operated for several decades by a kind of subterfuge—by the use of personnel on indefinite loan from various executive departments. Through the 1920's the Budget Bureau relied largely for its personnel on Army and Navy officers borrowed from the military service. While the Budget and Accounting Act of 1921 made the Budget Bureau, although nominally in the Treasury Department, a staff agency to serve the President directly, it was not until 1937 that anyone recommended that the President be given an Executive Office to include his principal staff agencies—particularly the White House Office and the budget, personnel, and planning agencies. This was the proposal of the President's Committee on Administrative Management.

The Hoover Commission built on the foundations of the report of the President's Committee, and it found no fault with the general theory of that report. Indeed, it went further along the same lines; for example, while the President's Committee suggested that the Budget Bureau undertake a program for the improvement of government management, the Hoover Commission recommended that that program be increased and strengthened.

With all the weight of its bipartisan membership, moreover, the Hoover Commission recommended that the President be given greater discretionary authority over the organization and operations of the Executive Office. Thus it proposed that statutory authority over operating departments should not be granted to any part of the President's office but only to the President himself, that the President should have authority to reorganize his Executive Office, and that all its members should be appointed by the President without confirmation by the Senate. These recommendations are hardly necessary to establish the President's authority over his own office. They serve rather to prevent the staff agencies from encroaching on the executive departments by controlling the details of operations.

Any staff agency, of course, is tempted to ask for some statutory functions of its own. Staff officers are not exempt from the human weakness of wanting more power. But it is easy to see what happens if this tendency is pushed very far. If a staff agency gets in the habit of asking the Congress for powers of its own, it is sure to begin to take orders from some congressional committee rather than from the President. Moreover, a staff agency is helpful to the President as long as it is small enough and compact enough to know what the President wants and to do the staff work to help him get it. If it gets big enough so that it becomes an elaborately organized institution, it may be almost as hard for the President to control as are the executive departments themselves. Nobody has yet worked out a formula to decide where you reach the point of diminishing returns, but the recommendations of the Hoover Commission would establish a rule of thumb that would help keep the Executive Office within its proper boundaries.

The failure of much of our scholarly research to appreciate the nature of our presidential system is best illustrated by its approach to the problem of the President as a legislative leader. Many of our books that deal with this subject seem completely unaware that most congressional committees *ask* the advice of the executive departments concerned before considering any legislation, that congressional leaders insisted that the Bureau of the Budget help the President co-ordinate the legislative program of the executive branch, or that the Budget Bureau has developed a procedural system for this purpose that reflects the realities of responsibility under the presidential system. That is a system of political relativity, in which the degree of the President's control over a department's legislative recommendations depends on many things—on the importance of the policy, the strength of regional sentiments, the current influence of party discipline, the importance of professional or scientific considerations, and the degree of outside support for the department in question. All these are balanced in a multidimensional system, in which a congressional committee is free to get the independent opinions of every politician or general or civil servant in the government, but in which the President is still the legislative leader of the nation.

[103]

On departmental organization, on reorganization power, and on executive staff the 1949 report of the Commission on Organization broke no new ground. It merely reaffirmed, and stated more boldly, the trend of thinking of the past several decades. But on a fourth point it dealt with a problem which is new in degree if not in kind, since the President's Committee on Administrative Management reported in 1937. This is the problem of organizing not for the execution of policy but to co-ordinate the development or formulation of policy.

The Committee on Administrative Management, and earlier the National Emergency Council, made a study of the problem of interdepartmental committees. But during the past decade, especially because of the need for a unified policy in international affairs, a much greater number of committees, including Cabinet members and agency heads, have been created to advise the President.

For example, the American Joint Chiefs of Staff was created only after the American generals and admirals were thrown together in the Combined Chiefs of Staff and began to discover that they were always disagreeing with each other, while the British members presented a united front. Similarly, the most important Cabinet committees were organized because the executive departments found themselves operating with their usual degree of semi-independence in international affairs. Each of them discovered with some surprise that it was acting as an independent principality—with a great deal more power than many a modern nation—in the hard and difficult business of diplomacy.

The difficulties that such a situation brought about were obvious. The remedy that was adopted could not be simply to make each department subordinate to the State Department in international matters. International and domestic problems were too closely linked for that. The remedy was rather to set up a series of Cabinet and interdepartmental committees, roughly paralleling the structure of the specialized international organizations. As the operating departments found that they would have to fit into the framework of unified policy, they very properly were interested in advising the President on what that policy should be, rather than having him act entirely upon the advice of his personal staff. Several of the department heads were enthusiastic about these Cabinet committees as a new means of co-ordinating top policy. Out of their wartime observation of the British government, and a great admiration of its close co-ordination, they began to advocate for the United States a Cabinet secretariat on the British model.

One fundamental difference, however, distinguishes the British committee technique from the American. The British, who understand that no system of co-ordination could work except on a flexible administrative basis, officially keep the very existence of their several Cabinet committees a secret. If a private member of the House of Commons inquires what kind of a committee is working on what problem, a Cabinet spokesman will tell him that it is none of his business. Moreover, the Cabinet Secretariat is only nominally an agency of the Cabinet —in effect it is a part of the Prime Minister's staff. This staff's shrewd management of committees (helping the Prime Minister determine the membership of committees, what subjects should go to what committee, and when each item should be brought up for discussion) is one of the features that lets the whole Cabinet system operate without voting.

But in the United States we are naïve enough not to accept the Bagehot idea that the effective organization of the government must operate behind a dignified or formal façade. As soon as Cabinet committees are created, their committees, their secretariats, and the interested congressional committees all want to give the Cabinet committees statutory status and statutory powers. And that in turn means that the committee secretariats are in a constant jurisdictional feud with the other committees and with the President's staff agencies. All this brings about a system not of co-operation but of active rivalry. It is more difficult for the President to co-ordinate a series of formalized committees and to keep them from overlapping and competing with one another than it is to co-ordinate the departments themselves.

The Hoover Commission might have dealt with this problem by proposing something like the British Cabinet Secretariat, or something like the recent Office of War Mobilization and Reconversion. Perhaps it did not suggest the former for fear that, like the latter, it would start by being merely a creature of the President and then have statutory status thrust on it by the Congress.

Instead of adding to the tangle of such statutory agencies, the Commission proposed to clarify responsibility by making the President free to manage them in his own discretion. It proposed that the President be given full authority to determine the membership and agenda of any Cabinet committee. (In particular, it applied these principles to the National Security Council and the National Security Resources Board.) Finally, the Commission recognized that the President needed staff assistance to enable him to guide and direct the Cabinet committees and to keep them from working in conflict with each other or with the staff agencies in the Executive Office. It accordingly recommended that the President have a Staff Secretary for this purpose but made it clear that the work of any such Staff Secretary must be completely under the discretionary guidance of the President himself.

This problem is not likely to be solved by the creation of a single secretariat. The pace of American politics is too fast, and the legislative program is too little under the influence of the chief executive to permit the public business to be co-ordinated in a completely orderly fashion. But a great deal of progress can be made, and to some extent is being made today in a very quiet and inconspicuous way, by developing habits of teamwork and internal clearance within the Executive Office. Most of the major policies and programs that have been developed for the President in the past year have been prepared by a group of officials from the executive departments concerned, under the guidance of staff members of the White House itself and other parts of the Executive Office. After preliminary work by junior staff members, some member of the Executive Office designated by the President—in the case of the anti-inflation program, for example, it was the chairman of the Council of Economic Advisers—has then revised the plan in consultation with Cabinet officials concerned and presented it with their varying advice to the President for decision.

The purpose of the Hoover Commission recommendations on the Presidency is to make this kind of flexible co-operation possible. It is not possible so long as there is not a clear line of responsibility to the President from all parts of the executive branch. Executive committees have worked poorly in the United States government simply because committee members too often have enough statutory or political independence so that they are inclined not to work out an agreement but rather to take their case separately to the public or to congressional committees.

The new administrative authority and machinery which the Hoover Commission proposes to give the President would give him no additional power over any private citizen. Nor are they designed to take power away from the Congress and to give it to the President. Quoting Alexander Hamilton, the Commission took the view that the responsibility of the President to the people, and the ability of the Congress to hold the executive branch accountable, would be increased by making executive leadership more energetic and unified. It is the power that lodges at low points in the executive hierarchy that is hardest to bring to light and hold effectively accountable.

The general significance of the Hoover Commission proposals, therefore, is this: the Commission rejected the logic that our system of checks and balances creates a fundamental conflict of interest between the President and the Congress; accordingly, the Commission made recommendations that were designed to increase the ability of the Congress and the President to work together to make the executive branch into an integrated whole and to reduce the irresponsible power of individual bureaus and pressure groups.

For in spite of all the looseness of our presidential system, and in spite of the internal stresses that develop among its regional and factional and jurisdictional interests, it has had two great advantages. It provides firmness and stability of government at times when internal disagreements are so bitter that no legislative majority could be assembled in support of a strong government of any description. And at all times the President, because he is free to set national goals by a direct appeal to the people, provides a more positive and nationally representative leadership than would ever be tolerated by a Cabinet that has to be sensitive to factional and regional interests.

Every great power that abolished its hereditary monarchy has found the parliamentary system the path to instability of government. The breakdown of the German Republic and the chronic anarchy of the French Republic suggest that when the United States gave up its loyalty to a dynasty it did well to create a new executive directly and constitutionally responsible to the people as a whole.

At the same time, the story of the more firmly disciplined parliamentary systems of the British Commonwealth makes it clear that the extension of democracy in such a parliamentary system means the end of the legislative assembly as a body that can amend and determine important measures of policy, each on its merits. As a result, the legislature is squeezed into compliance between a tightly integrated bureaucracy and a tightly organized party. And then the situation favors a process of nationalization—nationalization of industry and the extension of national control over provinces or municipalities.

A pluralistic society protects the great values of freedom. In it a citizen does not have to be ruled by an ideology or by any party or priesthood that is built on an ideology. He can side with one party on one issue and with its opponents on another.

In a unitary state, rooted in the traditions of a single nation, it is certainly possible to preserve pluralism in society without having checks and balances, as Americans know them, within the formal framework of government. In Great Britain today, for example, the trade unions and the professional and trade associations may already be a part of the effective constitutional system—as integral a part, and as effective in the defense of individual and group rights, as were the barons and bishops and burgesses and knights when they had been called together to help raise the royal revenue and were in the process of becoming a Parliament. But in a country that includes many races and nationalities, many cultures, and great regional diversity, there is less disposition to be deferential to tradition, and more disposition to push political controversy to its most unfortunate logical conclusions. In such a complex society, the institutional apparatus that seems best suited to the preservation of a pluralistic society is federalism plus a separation of powers.

The United States is the only free federal republic

among the great nations. The Presidency is the keystone of the system and helps maintain its federalism, its flexibility, and its freedom from ideological intolerance.

These features of federalism and separation of powers make for a certain amount of political looseness and administrative disorder. On the other hand, they make it more possible to accommodate various nationalities and cultures within the same effective system of government. And the lessons we have learned from our federal experience, by showing us how we may decide each issue less in the light of party ideology and more on the grounds of objective or even scientific criteria, may help us construct a more stable world order and break down the philosophical barrier that divides the nations.

In the meantime the President of the United States must be a world leader if the issue is drawn between freedom and tyranny. He deserves the co-operation of the Congress and the support of the electorate in making the executive branch a manageable organization. To strengthen his administrative authority along the lines recommended by the Hoover Commission would not only strengthen the unity of our national purpose, but make our whole system of federalism and free institutions stronger and more responsive to the highest purposes of the American people.

5

The Formulation of

American Foreign Policy

❦

❦ By Edgar Ansel Mowrer *

I N HIS inaugural address of January 20, 1949, a much-
moved President of the United States concentrated on
the world situation. "Each period of our national history," he said, "has had its special challenges." This is
an "eventful, perhaps decisive, period for us and the
world. . . . The peoples look to the United States for
good will, strength and leadership." Most nations, the
President went on to say, want a world of freedom,
peace, and "a decent and satisfying life." They are,
however, opposed by nations imbued with a "false philosophy" which is "communism—the opposite of democracy."

The American program for world peace and freedom
is, the President said, being based on "four major courses
of action": (1) unfaltering support of the United Nations;
(2) continued effort for world economic recovery, seeking
greater production and avoiding imperialism; (3)
"strengthening freedom-loving nations as against the
dangers of aggression" by such means as the Rio Pact
of 1947 and a North Atlantic Pact; (4) pooling our tech-
nical knowledge and industrial know-how with those
of other free peoples and encouraging capital investment in areas needing development.

In other words, the President's inaugural was, for the

* Edgar Ansel Mowrer, long time foreign correspondent of the
Chicago Daily News, Deputy Director of the Office of War
Information, and author of *The Nightmare of American Foreign
Policy* and other books, is at present a Washington columnist.

[115]

first time in American history, a recognition of the supremacy of foreign policy in our national life.

There is nothing very surprising in this recognition. Shortly after the Potsdam meeting in 1945, Mr. Truman told me personally that he intended to have a coherent world-wide foreign policy. This was initiated early in 1947 with the Truman Doctrine and was continued with the Marshall Plan. In his inaugural such a policy came to fruition. What is more, with his four-point program, President Truman was accepting what he called the "special challenges" of our historical period—as he understands them.

Behind the four objectives listed in Mr. Truman's inaugural address lies a more precise plan. This plan, the real kernel of present American foreign policy, has not been widely revealed and is still unrecognized by the American people. It was foreshadowed but certainly not clearly stated in the famous article by Mr. X (George F. Kennan of the State Department) entitled "The Sources of Soviet Conduct," which appeared in the July, 1947 issue of *Foreign Affairs*. It is simply that the United States and its friends shall keep the Soviet bloc under concentric pressure on a relatively limited front. American resources are not unlimited, and very little financial, economic, and military help is now available in other countries. Therefore, many possible areas must be neglected by us. The President's chosen pressure front stretches from the Arctic Ocean across Europe to the Mediterranean and into Iran, with special emphasis on certain areas like Germany and the Dardanelles. It may be summed up in a phrase that reads like a combined bridge and chess problem: "West to play and checkmate East in two to three years."

Within this period, the President believes, the various societies under Soviet rule, lacking help from the West, will go from bad to worse. Growing economic need and political dissatisfaction will eventually produce a series of explosions leading either to the collapse of the Soviet government or a world-wide political settlement. In other words, the President's expectancy of coming Soviet economic collapse is a sort of western counterpart to the Communist belief in a coming American depression. Each side believes that the other will crack first.

Because the President believes that he can obtain this result quickly, he is making certain terrific gambles. He is permitting the partial restoration of German economic power in order to keep the good will of the Germans. He is keeping up the so far not very productive economic and military aid to Greece. He is persisting in an effort to prop up the essentially feeble Arab states of the Middle East. His State Department is reluctant to take an all-out position against the Dutch in Indonesia, since we need Dutch assistance in Europe, and Asiatic problems can wait. The President condoned what looked like the abandonment of China to the Communists. He seems to accept the lame official explanation that Mao Tse-tung and his friends "will probably turn out to be Trotskyites." Finally, if he is worried about the division of Korea and the standstill position in Japan, he is not showing it.

Here Mr. Truman's attitude is logical. For if, within the next two years, the United States and its friends are able to make the Soviet Union choose between internal collapse and a general settlement on our terms, then why worry about other problems or areas which will be part of that settlement? The President and his advisers

[117]

seem convinced that they have here an efficient, practical, and relatively cheap plan. They are pursuing it regardless of the obviously terrible risks it invites if it fails to bring quick results.

It has long been recognized that it is difficult for a democracy to have a coherent foreign policy. It has even been argued that the greater the democracy, the greater the difficulty. It has been said that lacking certain necessary diplomatic tools—secrecy, dispatch, the possibility of quick tactical shifts and military bluffs, the cynical elimination of ideological and moral considerations—no policy makers can achieve anything serious. President Wilson apparently thought it impossible for a democracy successfully to clash diplomatic weapons with a despotism. It is in this sense that we must understand his insistence on making "the world safe for democracy."

Recent administrations have been extremely active and have already brought about changes in our traditional concepts which awaken both popular resistance and popular approval. The most notable is a shift to a totally new sort of semipublic diplomacy. Even when American policy abroad was largely limited to the traditional instructions, "observe, analyze, report," American practice largely followed "classical conceptions" and established habits. Of these secrecy was the most important. Keeping faith with other governments took precedence over informing one's own people—including the legislative branch of the United States government. As a result, the American Senate took an almost obscene pleasure in rejecting most treaties and agreements submitted by the President. The citizens were, save in conspicuous cases like the acceptance or repudiation of membership in Wilson's League of Nations, generally

[118]

uninterested. This has now been radically changed. Wherever possible, the administration either channels its aims through the United Nations or seeks in some way to tie them up with that organization. Public voting and appeal to the high court of public opinion are matters of course. These shock conservative members of the foreign service. They have been steadily utilized, more than ever, by Secretary Acheson.

As a background to any successful policy, there are certain basic needs. Among them are:

1. Ample information from all parts of the world and diplomats with enough understanding of foreign psychologies to interpret this information correctly. In this respect, during the last three years, improvement in the quality of the American foreign service has been notable. More and more keen minds have entered the service. Abroad, they have adopted tactics more like those of reporters on a continuing assignment than of conventional diplomats. From social contacts with the leaders of the country where they are stationed, they have extended their efforts to its business, labor, publicity, and culture groups. The result has been a marked improvement in the gathering and interpretation of information from abroad.

2. A just estimate of the domestic situation. Obviously no policy can succeed beyond the financial and economic resources available for backing it up. Statesmen must also correctly appraise popular opinion. A friend of mine in the State Department remarks that "in our democracy it is better to debate an issue without settling it than to settle it without a debate." Policy makers must also have full knowledge of the ever-present special influences and lobbies.

There is, for instance, no doubt that a Catholic lobby influenced the unhappy American decision against arming the Spanish Republic in the thirties and still protects Spain's dictator, Francisco Franco. The Jewish (and pro-Jewish) lobby recently turned out to be stronger than the pro-Arab lobby backed by the big oil companies and helped bring about an American decision favorable to Israel.

The rule seems to be that where the public is indifferent, a private lobby can be decisive, but where the people's convictions about anything are strong, no lobby can successfully oppose them.

Moreover, in the United States, any successful policy must have the consensus of the Senate and the House of Representatives. Almost any foreign political line leads at some point to a treaty with other powers. In this instance, the Senate is omnipotent. Most observers agree that Mr. Roosevelt's wartime policy of keeping a group of bipartisan senators "in the know" was absolutely vital in bringing about quasi-unanimous acceptance of the United Nations Charter by the Senate. Administration-sponsored trial balloons like the B2H2 Resolution in the Senate and the Fulbright Resolution in the House of Representatives helped mightily. It can be argued that Arthur Vandenberg's "conversion" to internationalism early in 1945 was the direct result of the Roosevelt "contact." Without Vandenberg's support much, perhaps most, of the present Truman policy would not have been adopted.

Moreover, so many present policies demand economic or financial support that the acquiescence of the House of Representatives in the administration's wishes has become almost as important as that of the Senate. Hence the House Committee on Foreign Affairs, formerly a sort of "attic committee" in which the representatives who did not specially qualify for something else found themselves, has been propelled into the foreground, and members actually seek to be assigned to it. It can be counted on increasingly not only to influence but, by indirect methods, even to initiate policy.

The recent designation of an Assistant Secretary of State for the sole purpose of maintaining harmonious relations between the State Department and the Capitol is evidence of the new trend. Of course, the exact amount of information that can safely be given to the lawmakers by the administration is hard to determine. One can, however, sympathize with the Secretary of State who once said, "If you tell 'em too little they go fishing, if you tell 'em too much they go crazy." The American Congress, we must never forget, has always been thoroughly imbued with the sacred need for opposing the executive.

Against such a background, real policy making in the United States usually starts in the State Department. A typical case was that of the Truman Doctrine. When the British announced that they were bankrupt and unable to continue assisting Greece and Turkey, the State Department had to make a decision. George F. Kennan was brought down from the War College for a special meeting by the then Under Secretary, Dean Acheson. After listening to the situation, Mr. Kennan urged American shouldering of what had been a British responsibility. The plan was thoroughly examined and approved by the relevant bureaus. Then it was accepted by the new Secretary of State, General George Marshall. When he had made up his mind, it was sold to the President of the United States.

President Truman realized that no such radical break with American tradition as this projected interference in Europe in time of peace could possibly succeed without the support of Congress. Therefore he invited an important group of Senators and Representatives to confer with him at the White House. At the most important of these meetings, the decision was put squarely up to Senator Vandenberg. The Senator finally answered, "Mr. President, I'll support it if you explain it to the Congress and to the people of the United States."

In considering how he might explain the proposal, the President saw three possible ways. He finally decided to wrap American aid to Greece and Turkey within a general principle of giving American assistance to all countries struggling to remain free. The outcome was the historical act called the Truman Doctrine, presumably the most important in American history since the Monroe Doctrine over a century before.

One paragraph in President Truman's speech to the Congress underlined the paramount use of economic aid. This became the germ of the Marshall Plan which was completely to transform the situation of western Europe. Yet—a most extraordinary feature—the Marshall Plan was enunciated by the Secretary of State before it had really been worked out in the minds of its authors. General Marshall got around this difficulty by cleverly suggesting that the European countries involved work out the details for themselves. The same sort of indirection was followed in the early negotiations for the North Atlantic Security Pact a year later. In both cases, American-born babies were handed to Europe to nurse.

It has now become normal for a policy to originate

in the Policy Planning Staff of the State Department, whence it goes directly to the Secretary and then to the relevant bureaus. At every stage of the formulation of a new objective, the President and the State Department face several problems. One of these is timing—when exactly to consult the interested foreign governments, the Congress, and the people. Should the State Department, for instance, first seek to reach an agreement with the other governments potentially involved before "leaking" the idea to the public and confiding in the Senate Committee on Foreign Relations? If it does so, it risks the charge of "seeking to commit the country without the consent of the people and the Congress." Or should the President first publicly outline an aim, then discuss its concrete content with chosen senators and, having won their assent, open negotiations with other countries? In this case, these other governments are likely to complain of "American blackmail." Making an unrealized policy public in advance gives enemies, both domestic and foreign, a chance to kill it. Keeping it secret until it is almost realized invites the risk of repudiation at home. These and a dozen similar problems are involved in "timing."

Another type of difficulty lies in the administrative anarchy—at least the absence of adequate organization —within the State Department itself. Frequently it has seemed that the best advice that could be given to any American Secretary of State was to sign absolutely no document or letter whose origin and purposes were not crystal-clear to him and concerning which all the relevant facts had not been furnished.

Another recent problem is the overweening influence of the military in foreign affairs. During World War II, as Secretary Hull has revealed in his memoirs, the State Department virtually abdicated to the armed services. President Roosevelt took an almost childish pleasure in by-passing his State Department and keeping his Secretary of State in the dark about his real plans. Shrewd foreign statesmen like Winston Churchill were quick to take advantage of this. For instance, in the early summer of 1944, Britain through Ambassador Halifax sought Secretary Hull's consent to division of the Balkans into "spheres of influence." Hull flatly refused; whereupon Churchill secretly obtained Roosevelt's consent.

This by-passing of the State Department transferred a good deal of work to other persons and agencies. Some of it was carried out by the "Deputy President" of the United States, Harry Hopkins. But much inevitably devolved upon the military. Secretary of War Stimson saw no wrong in this. It was from the Joint Chiefs of Staff, not from the State Department, that the President in 1941 obtained the "memorandums" concerning the kind of world the United States wanted after the war. General Marshall seems to have been responsible for Roosevelt's flat refusal to consider the invasion of Europe through the Balkans rather than in western France. Admiral Leahy, a very amateur diplomat indeed, was part author of the plan for keeping contact with Vichy and using non-Gaullist Frenchmen. Eisenhower rather than Hull conducted the negotiations that got Italy out of the war while saddling the United Nations with Marshal Badoglio—a move that had important political consequences.

Since the war, no Secretary of State has had the courage to resume full responsibility for foreign policy in all areas of the world. Lacking experience, President

Truman turned naturally to those eminent Americans of whom he had heard the most. In wartime this meant the generals and admirals. Moreover, for General George Marshall, Mr. Truman had an almost filial respect. As Secretary of State, General Marshall continued to look on political problems as military first of all. Thus, while to a certain extent he kept the ambitious Pentagon in order, inevitably his choice of assistants fell upon people, both military and civilian, with whose work he was familiar. Under Secretary of State Lovett had served in the War Department.

The President cluttered up important diplomatic posts with high brass and for years left the two all-important occupied areas under American proconsuls, Generals Clay and MacArthur. With the President inexperienced in foreign matters and the State Department unwilling to reassert its authority, the men in uniform who knew what they wanted and were not afraid of responsibility naturally continued to boss the show.

Moreover, Mr. Truman and General Marshall found in the Congress plenty of "people's representatives" who had more confidence in the brass that won the war than in the President's political appointees. Finally, at Marshall's suggestion, Congress set up the all-important National Security Council. This body was purely advisory and, in theory, concerned with purely military matters. Members were, however, the Secretary of State (the *sole* civilian) and the *four* military Secretaries (Defense, Army, Navy, Air). Since practically every postwar foreign problem had a "defense angle," the Council regularly found itself passing on political issues. Final decisions must be taken by the President. Yet I have not heard of any case where President Truman has overridden the judgment of this almost exclusively military body.

Here let us open a parenthesis to ask: What is the purpose of any foreign policy, and When can it be considered adequate? To the first question two easy answers are commonly given—the one hard-boiled, the other sentimental. The first runs: "To protect the country's vital interests"; the second: "To further right and justice." Any successful democratic policy must incorporate the first answer and at least appear to incorporate the second.

The answer to the second question is complicated. The policy of any country in a multistate system begins with what might be called *basic purposes*. In the United States, these may be defined as: (1) the maintenance of freedom, both without and within the country; (2) the safeguarding of peace; and (3) the promotion of ever-increasing abundance.

The first two are permanent. The third is essentially dynamic. Americans are rich but expect to be richer. The promises contained in President Truman's 1949 address to the Congress on the State of the Union—more benefits for everybody—are typical.

Adequacy of a foreign policy means, in the first instance, that the *basic purposes* are being steadily pursued. If not, something is wrong.

Next after *basic purposes* come *appropriate objectives*. President Truman's main objective—as we have seen—is forcing a solution with the Soviet Union which will prevent the spread of Communism. Objectives are sought by long-term moves such as the Truman Doctrine, Marshall Plan, the Rio Pact uniting Latin American defense, the North Atlantic Security Pact—while maintaining the United Nations and seeking a satisfactory solution of the atomic energy problem. And finally, there are the thousands of short-term, day-to-day decisions on matters of detail.

Quite obviously, *basic purposes* cannot be invented by any administration and cannot be planned. They spring from the nature of a people. *Appropriate objectives* must be tailored to the available cloth, in both material and ideal, or they cannot be pursued.

Finally, in a democracy, any adequate policy must, in my judgment, be capable of simple, acceptable expression and coherent pursuit. Too great subtlety leads to popular confusion and lack of interest. National wobbling invites popular repudiation. It dismays friends and heartens enemies. The worst that can happen to any country is a reputation for unreliability.

The time has come for a brief consideration of the degree of inadequacy, not of foreign policy in general but of the policy that is now being offered the American people. In my judgment, President Truman's conduct of our foreign affairs is open to criticism on two counts—first, as to execution, and second, as to the scope of its objectives.

Practically no one who lives in day-to-day touch with our foreign policy makers doubts that the present conduct of our foreign affairs still lacks coherence and a sense of responsibility. This lack has resulted, among other things, in such weaknesses as the brusque changes of front on the disposition of the Italian colonies, the future of Germany, the division and frontiers of Palestine, and our proper attitude toward the Argentine Republic. Irresponsibility accounts for the contradictory public utterances concerning the place of Spain within or without the North Atlantic Security Pact. It explains why the Marshall Plan was publicly announced before anybody in Washington knew exactly what was intended.

Deficiencies in organization have resulted in allowing the policy to be made in too many separate government agencies. A typical result was the recent statement, subsequently but not convincingly denied, by former Secretary of the Army Kenneth Royall that the United States intends to pull out of Japan. The same imbalance resulted in the diverting but not profitable spectacle of General Lucius Clay in Berlin being permitted to work against the top diplomats in Washington. It produces the appalling wobbles of the United States delegation at the United Nations with the resulting loss in American prestige.

It has been hard to convince some people in Washington that the United States has become too influential to permit itself any further to proceed by the time-honored system of trial and error. When our master voice croaks in public cacophony, it is no longer diverting—it is devastating. Not even the United States is rich enough to afford the traditional luxury of pitting inexperienced and naïve political appointees against an old master like Molotov at the diplomatic chessboard. This, James Byrnes, while Secretary of State, learned to his cost. The American people will have to learn the same lesson. On the field of world affairs our most experienced champions are none too good.

Such typical deficiencies are, however, the growing pains of world leadership. Most of them could, I believe, be cured by the recent recommendations of the Hoover

Commission. Roughly speaking, these would concentrate full responsibility for foreign relations in the State Department. Within that Department they would restore predominant influence to the *political* as opposed to the *functional* officials. Above all, they would establish a direct chain of command with adequate staff services, thanks to which responsibility could be traced at all levels. This in turn might make it possible (after all, anything is possible in Washington) to silence or punish those officials who "talk out of turn" on matters of state.

On one point I dissent strongly from the Hoover recommendations. Unfortunate, in my judgment, would be an immediate amalgamation of the present foreign service of the United States with the present State Department people. The former are highly trained specialists, the latter at best amateurs, even when highly gifted. Before any such amalgamation can usefully occur, the State Department people should also receive specialized training equal to that given the foreign service. As I read American history, fuzzy minds and blinkered functionalists have done far more damage than "striped pants."

I would, moreover, amend the Hoover recommendations in the sense of even further reducing direct military influence on the formulation of foreign policy. In an unhappy era like ours, the military have and will continue to have a place in international affairs. Yet, save for a few exceptionally gifted individuals, they are unfitted to make political policy. Their whole training unfits them. In this I agree with Professor Hans Morgenthau, who writes in his *Politics among Nations:*

No nation can pursue a policy of compromise with the military determining the ends and means of foreign policy. The armed forces are instruments of war. . . .

[129]

The objective of war is clear and simple and uncondi-
tional: to break the will of the enemy. . . . The sole question before [the military leader] is how to win victories as
cheaply and quickly as possible and how to avoid defeat. . . .

To surrender the conduct of foreign affairs to the military
then is to destroy the possibility of compromise and thus to
surrender the cause of peace. . . . A foreign policy conducted by military men according to the rules of the military
art can only end in war. . . .[1]

One might have thought this had been written in
reference to the present situation at Berlin. Yet at the
end of 1947 I saw the man responsible for the Berlin
impasse, General Lucius Clay, who reports only to the
War Department, actually change the policy of the
American delegation at London toward Germany, although the State Department had in Germany a full-
rank (though permanently fledgling) ambassador,
Robert Murphy. Placing all political responsibility for
occupied areas under the State Department and reducing the commanders there to housekeepers and chiefs of
police is long overdue.

As a further step toward eliminating military influence, I would suggest the reorganization of the National
Security Council. One voice, that of the Secretary of
Defense, should be loud enough to express the opinions
of the armed services. Place should be made for the
Secretaries of Commerce and of the Treasury. With the
Secretary of State they would constitute three civilians
against one military representative, a proper proportion
for a democracy. Nothing need prevent the Secretaries

---

[1] New York: A.A. Knopf, 1948, pp. 442–443.

of the three forces from attending meetings as advisers, along with the appropriate functionaries from the State Department and the director of central intelligence.

Going slightly beyond the Hoover recommendations, I would make one or two further suggestions. Both the recommended Deputy Under Secretaries of State should be made permanent and handsomely paid. They are the only guarantees of the coherence and continuity of whatever foreign policy exists. Then, too, it would be well to add to the Policy Planning Staff a few newsmen and businessmen as permanent advisers. With becoming modesty I should point out that the former at least have a record in foreseeing international developments that can more than bear comparison with that of the diplomats.

Concerning certain obvious needs I have nothing to suggest. For nothing short of a constitutional amendment could free the President (perhaps by the creation of two or even three Vice-Presidents) for the job of steering the ship of state in foreign waters. Nor dare one hope for any real improvement in the relations between the State Department and Congress. Here, too, short of a change to a parliamentary system of government, we can expect the present unhappy "special relation" (half co-operation, half rivalry) to continue unabated. The chasm between the two effected under George Washington is far too deep to be easily bridged, for it was dug by the makers of the American Constitution.

It is, however, permissible to point out that in gambling the future safety of the United States on a quick bloodless victory over the Soviet Union, President Truman is going farther than is necessary. I do not imply that the objective is wrong. Quite the contrary. But any policy that ignores the latent dangers of a resurgent, aggressive Germany and a sacrificed Asia is needlessly perilous. If it fails, it will make World War III in more adverse circumstances all but inevitable.

My second criticism of our present foreign policy is directed not at its conduct but at the scope of its objectives. These are, in my judgment, too narrow. Containment of Communism and a settlement with the Soviet Union are simply not enough. Nor can the deficiency be made up by a verbal deference to the manifestly ill-framed United Nations.

In his inaugural address the President implied his intention of meeting the "great challenges" of our time. But he overlooked the main challenge. This, I submit, is not Communism. Containing aggression is necessary, but if America's basic purposes of freedom, peace, and ever-increasing abundance are to be well served, then a much greater step is required. This is the elimination of war and the fear of war from the planet.

Failure to achieve this, even if the present strategy leads to a normal settlement between the United States and the U.S.S.R., would still leave room for an equally normal air-and-atom armament race. For this is inherent in the multination system. Any such race will chisel away domestic freedom and reduce living standards. Symptoms of both losses are already present. I refer to the so-called Communist spy hysteria and to the size of our military appropriation. And at the end of an armament race is the probability of the kind of war whose outcome no man can foresee.

To me, at least, it is clear that until war and the fear of war are eliminated, humanity, far from advancing, will be able to do nothing more than mark time and wait for a break. Those great social and economic objectives which theoretically are for the very first time obtainable on earth will remain unreached. In its failure to work positively for permanent peace lies the grave defect of the otherwise brave Truman policy. Merely wishing for peace is not enough. The ills of one period cannot be cured with the remedies of a preceding one. Failure here is another ghastly example of what I have called the nightmare of American foreign policy.

War and the fear of war can be eliminated one way only, namely, by the constitution of a permanent preponderance of power and the substitution of law for arbitrary violence. This is not the place to indicate the appropriate steps. Suffice it to remark that once the President recognized the validity of the aim and the principle, means would not fail him. Such a recognition —public, of course—by Harry S. Truman would change the international picture overnight.

Here is a method that would make American leadership accepted wherever men, weary of the ancient ritual of man-made disaster and convinced that the next calamity will be the worst, are looking for something radical and new.

At the third United Nations Assembly last year it was generally recognized that the existing world organization did not and could not fulfill expectations. Yet two delegations remained conspicuously silent on this point, those of the United States and Russia. The Soviets had their own good motives, their scheme for eliminating war by creating a World Union of Socialist Soviet Republics. The United States delegation was moved by no such great ambition, merely by lack of imagination. Certain members of the State Department do indeed recognize the need for transforming the United Nations into something better and inaugurating a foreign policy to end all foreign policy, but unfortunately they do not shape our policy.

Yet everywhere in the world people are waiting and hoping to see the American policy evolve and grow. They see the new challenge, though our President ignores it. Either the physicists have given us a new epoch, or they have not. If they have, as most thoughtful people concede, then a new policy must be devised to meet the new challenge. Peace, next only to liberty, is the all-important need. Therefore, the pursuit of peace by truly adequate methods must be direct. Since we live in a two-story world—an old world dying below, a young one being born above—American leaders must for a time continue to work on both levels. On the old level of power politics backed by armed force the main tasks are indeed containing Soviet imperialism and winning the cold war. But on the floor above, the job is of another nature—the creation of a political environment where mankind can finally be free to develop whatever possibility of a better life human brains can invent.

Here—as I see it—lies an unequaled opportunity for American leadership. If I believed in specific historical destinies, I would insist that just for this was the United States of America created.